Poems, Peoms

& Other Atrocities

Poems, Peoms
& Other Atrocities

Garry Kilworth
&
Robert Holdstock

*C*ontents

Life & Death

Nature

Others

The 'Crab' Poems

Peoms

$\mathcal{P}$reface

obert Paul Holdstock, 'Rob' to those who knew and loved him, died in November, 2009. He was the best of friends, a hugely talented writer of fiction, an inspiration, and a man who was happy to engage with anyone and everyone he met. He is massively missed by all his friends, who were many. His 'mythago' novels, a word he invented, are now deeply embedded in the psyche of the body general of fantasy fiction. Rob only started writing poetry, a few years before his death. He used a fluid, free style in the manner of one of his heroes, Walt Whitman and we shared a love of this great poet, along with Ted Hughes, WB Yeats and Tennyson. Beyond these four, we read our own separate ways, but often shared a newly discovered poem not of this quartet. Once Rob got in the flow of writing poems he would send them out to his friends and family, taking little notice of any adverse criticism. If you told him you were not that enamoured of his latest offering you would get two more back by return, with no apology attached.

I have written poetry since the age of 20, when I was incarcerated for a long year on Gan Island in the Maldives by the RAF. As a wireless operator I had little to do on this lonely desert island, half-a-mile square, except swim and read. There was a good library, however, and I read right through it, including a great many of the classics, developing a love of poetry on the way. I also began writing my own verses, which were naturally derivative at first, of all those poets I had come to admire. Much later, an exchange system developed between Rob and me. I would send him one of my latest attempts and he would respond with one of his. We even exchanged the sparks of ideas, to see what our different approaches could do with these small bright lights. He called me one day not long before he left us and said '"The iron wind", see what you can do with that, Gaz.' Readers of this volume will find those three words in one of his poems and in one of mine. 'Old age is a bull', I countered on another exchange. Rob actually used this in his last novel *Avilion* while with me it made another short poem. The phrase 'the iron wind' appears in his poem 'The Field of Tartan' about the Somme, and indeed in one or two others.

As freelance writers Rob and I would call each other two or three times a week. He phoned other writers too. He loved his 'creative thinking time' just as much as putting fingers to the keys, and his chats to others during the day were very important to him. He produced many fine novels and a number of great short stories and on several occasions in his emails, he said, 'We have to do a book of poems together, Gaz. We'll call it *Poems, Peoms and Other Atrocities* and include our peoms at the back.' (Rob coined the word 'peoms' to separate the humorous verses from the more serious stuff.) 'So,' I replied with the weighty pomp of a BA in English behind me, 'we're copying Wordsworth and Coleridge with their *Lyrical Ballads?*' There was a moment's silence, before he came back with, 'Emulating, Gaz, emulating.'

Shortly before his death Rob said to me, 'Faber and Faber, that's where we'll send *Atrocities.*' Now, Faber and Faber were our publishers, back in 1976 when our Editor there, Charles Monteith, took a chance on both of us and brought out our first novels. Charles has long since gone the way of great editors (he was the first to publish William Golding and was a colleague of TS Eliot, besides discovering Holdstock and Kilworth). Christopher Priest was already being published by Faber when they accepted Rob's first novel, then a little later my first, and not long afterwards

Christopher Evans joined us. They called the four of us the 'Faber Mafia' back in those heady days, when the world seemed to need to give 'movements' a colourful name. We were never a movement, but we were all good friends, and more importantly, remained so.

We are not being published by Faber and Faber, but by another great publisher with a smaller profile, who having missed the chance to discover Seamus Heaney, think they've got a runner up with the Kilworth and Holdstock anthology. So here they are, our poems: the shorter ones mine, the taller ones Rob's—in accordance with the physical statures nature gave us. Sarah and I decided to leave in those snippets of emails and notes which Rob attached to his poems when he sent them to his friends and family, adding that little extra 'Rob' touch.

Finally, this seems a good place to thank my good friend Sarah, Rob's partner for over 25 years. Sarah has spent many, many months tracking down Rob's poems. It would have been nice if they had all been in one place and each one neatly labelled 'Final Draft' but unfortunately Rob had no premonition of his death and in any case that was not his way. There were several versions of each and every poem, and all were scattered widely over the globe. Many were as elusive as snow leopards. But my co-worker was dogged in her search and here they all are. Sarah, thank you for your invaluable help.

—Garry Kilworth, 2012

Poems, Peoms

& Other Atrocities

For Annette and Sarah

War

The Field of Tartan

For my grandfather. He walked across this field on the Somme: July 1916.

—RH

I walked for my life, across a field of tartan.

The Scots went first. They had it worst.
The First, the Twenty-First.
Highlanders.
They sowed the seeds, the soft touch
Of fabric-woven earth, over which we walked.
They had been mown down to a man.

They made a field of tartan.

Before they went, they sang.
The songs were haunted.
We joked about their skirts; they took it in good part.
There was a sense of peace,
Resignation!
That touch of Spartan in each heart.

(He walks for his life, across a field of tartan.)

No mud when the top was crossed,
When the iron wind blasted and counter-crossed,
Seeking the marrowbone, the head, the heart,

Taking us down into that field of tartan.

It was so strange, so savage.
Astonishing to find no earth, just fallen flesh;
To briefly meet a dying gaze,
A last remembered highland day.
To walk over limbs clad in scarlet tartan.

And we slipped and slid upon the patterned cloth, but
    made the other line.
There was killing, then.

No charms, just arms, the sinking down, the frightened
   frown,
Flesh suddenly shaped into dirt, life dearth,
Blood silt,
Nothing to hearten us
Except our unwanted luck at walking over hand-weaved
   kilt.
Not sinking into earth.
Walking across a field of tartan.

RH, April 2008, revised September 2008

When I wrote this, last night, I cried.

My grandfather's account came back, very stark and strong. He lost a good few friends there. But the Scots... Good God!

I know the barrier's high when it comes to War Poetry. But we must constantly revisit it, it seems to me, through the lost dreams of those who were there.

—RH

Brief Lives

The average lifespan
of a Battle of Britain
fighter pilot
was 3 weeks,
a lot longer than
the 4 hours of
a soldier at Stalingrad,
and an aeon next to
that of a 2nd Lieutenant
'in country' Vietnam,
which was
15 minutes.

Consider the brevity
of the 30-minute mayfly,
which lives twice as long
as our Joe did,
once the army took him.

—GK

Haunted

The sailor sails,
The airman flies.
They see majesty and beauty
And the world
  With different eyes.

It turns, yet nothing turns.
Ice melts, ice grows,
Strange, haunted winds blow
  Across deserts, once forested and ferned.

All but the turning, turning, the endless turn,
Ends in the yearning for one day more.
Grasp that day.
  It will all end in the urn.

—RH

Jugged

This poem was inspired by Ted Hughes's 'Bayonet Charge'. Rob and I were stunned by Hughes's poem when we read it over Rob's kitchen table.

—GK

There was a moment:

He was sprawled across the wire,
Shot through, limb lost,
Thinking faintly of what might be higher
Than the iron barbs, keeping him so still, dead not,
Not yet,
A moment when a creature ran through No Man's Land.

A hare.

It had no business being there!

He was surprised it wasn't shot.
It stopped and looked at him. (God! The dawn was grey.)
It rose into that stark, cold, early morning,
Gun clatter sounded, but it didn't run away.
It stayed. Curious of face (hares can do that).
Missing his form? Or searching for some other place.
Somewhere quiet.

And the hare said to him:

'I am just a dying dream.
A memory from a time when it must have seemed, to you,
That life would last for ever.
By the way, your brother...
Over there, further down the line.

'He's gone away. You'll meet him soon.

'I was skinned, cooked, your grandmother
Did the deed.
A feast for the harvest moon.
My fate, the fate of all my kind,

11

To be slit, jugged and heated on the fire.

'Yours, you poor sod, to struggle on the wire.'

'I wonder why men bother?'

The Helmet

In some corner of a homeland field
a soldier's helmet lay, brimful of rainwater.
It saved the life of a lost and harried fox
who lapped and hurried on. It shaded an overheated
toad, who crawled beneath to cool its skin.
It was a life-giving lake to insects,
out in the barren wastes of a ploughed landscape,
and a bathing hole for dusty birds.
The man it was made for, wore it once, and died,
body shattered by a shell.
There are a hundred uses for a brick.

—GK, 2002

Crater Encounter

Under a three quarter moon,
Bright!
Though a ghost-mist obscured the clouds.
Stuck in a crater, legs useless,
But it was a silent night, and for a moment,
There was peace. The contemplation of that moon,
Shining on, despite the smoke.
Making life dangerous.
Twenty yards to death, twenty to home.
Stuck; no particular right to roam. No possibility.
Damned legs. No longer utility.
Nice moon though. Nice glow. Lie back and watch. Nice
   way to go.
But then: who's this?
Standing at the crater's edge, long hair flowing,
Beautiful, armoured, silver in the glowing moon,
Slipping down, now, down below the ridge,
Then standing, proud,
Speaking in a voice, confident, loud,
'You look like you could do with this.'
She's dressed like a knight of old, greaves of iron, breast-
   plate, skirt of mail,
Bright hair in full youth, bright smile,
She doesn't talk uncouth, but rather,
Frenchy.
No weapons: no sword, no spear, no halberd, arrow, bow
   or shear-edged knife.
Just a mug, a piece of clay, fired to shape, steaming.
'Thought you could do with this.'
'What is it?'
'Not sure. Tea or something. Something from before my
   time.'
'Tea?'
If she's right, what can I say? Sublime.
A cuppa. In the crater. Just the ticket.

'Thanks.'
I take a sip, then take a chance.
'You're Joan.'
'Yes. And you're in my France.'
'Didn't come here by choice, love. Dance of war. War dance.'
'I love my France,' she says, looking wistful, adding,
'It was on a night like this that I was taken to the pyre.
Left for hours before they put out the fire.
That ended me. My dream.
You English,
Put an end to me.
Flared in a flash,
Charred bone and ash.'
I gulp down tea, thinking of useless legs, thinking of twenty
   yards,
'Didn't have anything to do with it myself.'
'I know,' says Joan, and kisses me; soft and gentle; knowing.
   'It's history.'
Then she looks up at the moon. 'Grey ghost coming.'
She means a sniper. This is it, then. Slick, sharp slice of steel,
   and the crater is my grave.
Joan's gone. I hear a grunt, a moan. Grey ghost silenced.
And then her whisper, like a welcome wave,
'Legs gone, arms strong,
You're not tied to the stake. You can make it.
Other grey ghosts coming. You have seconds. To make the
   yards.
If this were a game of cards,
The hand is with you.'
'Both of them,' she adds.
The moon is bright.
I made it. Again I took the chance.
Crawling. Hands clutching clay, eager for the dance.
Thanks for cup of tea and courage, you ghost-lit memory of
   France.

—RH, 2007?

The Iron Wind

[In 1879 25000 Zulus charged into a hail of
fire from 2000 Martini-Henry rifles.
It was at a place called Isandlwana and after their
total victory the Zulu youths used the battle cry:
'We are the boys of Isandlwana'.]

We are the boys of Isandlwana
who faced the iron wind.
A furnace wind,
like the Saharan Simoom
or Haboob of Khartoum,
bringing madness on its breath.
No shield can turn it,
no mask,
no magic cloak.
Warriors are whisked away
like broken straws.
Sometimes
it takes our heads clean off.
We are the boys of Isandlwana
who race at the fiery rush,
into the bulleting blast,
for wind is only wind
and tomorrow the enemy
will be calm
and quiet
and utterly still.

—*GK*

Trench Ghost

'My name's Billy,' he says. 'You all right?'

It's night. Nearly dawn.
Where'd you come from, Billy?
We're a bit stuck here.

'Got to get you 'ome, right? Got to get you back to old
Blighty.'
We make such a joke of Blighty.
Yeah! Get us through the lines.

'No problem ... '
Says the Billy. And he winks.
'Just a few links in the chain,
To mend
Get you through.
No problem in the end.'

*My granddad haunts
me. I can hear his voice.
His stories, his calm, his
certainty, his affection. I
wish I'd known him
better.*

—RH

Pinned down, caught in a trench,
No wider than a butcher's bench,
Where pig or lamb are chopped,
Cut,
Given up, sectioned,
Hung on wire, displayed,
Dismayed,
That's us. Stuck in the bloody butcher's trench.

Now Billy!
Like a dream come true.
'It is my job!' Says he
(Proudly spoken, a little finger stabbing chest)

'To get yer 'ome, right?'
Right!
'Cos I knows the way. I done it before.
Trust me? If you trust me
I'll make sure
Your loving parents get to hug you, kiss you,
Welcome you back.
That's my business, see?
I knows the track. The lore,
The maps that tracks to home.
Hugging and kissing, and a good comfy bed
Made up for you in the corner, that's the lick,
For each and every one of you who's quick.'

Bleedin' Hun, got us pinned down.
We let Billy know the score.
'No frigging problem. What's my name?'
Billy, we echoes,
And he throws a quick laugh,
'That's me. Old Goat. Like Old Devil, right? A right sore.
I'll see you sorted bright and right! Not arsed!
Home, boys. The bed in the corner.
Good sleep, no more of the forlorn
Thinking!
Trust me.
It will have passed.'

What confidence that young man had.
Couldn't place him. Essex? Kent? Southern, yes.
Unlike us, not in a mess,
He just kept beckoning.
'This way lads.'
We followed.
Glad, to be led.

'This way lads.'
Through the enemy lines. Hun, with spiky helmet, machine
    gun,
Jesus effing Christ!

They didn't see us.
We crawled past,
Might have been mist, men of mist,
They missed us,
Ghosts, we were, in mud terrain,
Mud-drenched with blood and brain,
Crawled right through them.
Complain?
You've got to be fucking joking. How'd it happen?
No idea at all.
Thank god for Billy. He knew the way.
No need for God though. No need to pray.

So there we are. By the sea.
Over the sea?
I can't rhyme it. But Blight EE.
Good old Inga Land.

And there's me dad. And me mum. And Sis.
Funny kid, all shy and insecure.
'Welcome home son.'
That's dad.
He looks at me strange.
Mum looks at me with tears.
'Glad you got back,' she says
'Glad to be here.'
'We got your bed ready. In the corner.'
'Thanks. I'm ready for a rest.'

And the old boy says,
'Couldn't have lived without knowing what had happened.'
'Understand that,' says I. 'Billy got me home.'
'Billy?'
'He found us. In the trench. Brought us home.'
'Then thank you Billy, then,' says my dad.
He adds: 'Couldn't have lived, son. Not knowing.'
'That I know. The worst thing in everything
Is the not knowing.'
'Your bed's made up,' says he.

'In the corner. Yes. You told me. In the corner. Bed made
    up.'
'You want to rest?'
'Not yet,' says I.

The worst thing is not knowing.
The best thing is knowing . . .
Even though the best thing about knowing,
Is knowing the worst thing.

'That I know,' I tells him. I have nothing left to say.
'And I'm glad you know.'

'Things will change,' my daddy says,
'And life will proceed in the proper manner.
We'll have another boy. A girl perhaps.
We've life in us.
We know the proper manner.
Grief and tears, they'll never leave us.
Life and joy, always there to please us.
You did what you had to do.
You'll never go away.'

I know. I know. I wish I could have understood it better.

'A ghost returned,' says he, 'A touch. How can I tell you
That a kiss is better than a letter?
Words last, but are cold, so cold;
When I'm old
I'll love this moment of your passing,
Your short and certain walk to bed.
Having done your best
You go to rest.'

What is a father? I asks myself, as I contemplate the
    Sleeping.
He holds the sky in place. He holds the earth firm with his
    feet
Until it is time for the earth to move.

He moves with the moving earth,
His gentle look signals the change of season,
His smile the smile of farewell,
The knowingness of change.

'Your bed is made up.'
'Why is it made of oak? That costs too much.'
'Your bed is made up. Sleep when you will.'
'Brass handles?'
'We decided against candles. There will be enough candles
    in the church.'
'A small saving. But this is too much.'
'Why is it too much?'
'Why do I deserve oak?'
'What do you deserve, then? If not oak.'

I have no answer.
'I'm not ready to sleep. Not yet,' says I.
'Then stay and talk,' says he.

—*RH, November 2007*

Balance

In these quiet Suffolk Churchyards
are mounds of men at peace,
whose ordered lives were lived by rote.
The stones are every shape of sacred,
and planted in the unkempt earth
at every angle known to Man.

Over there, Normandy crosses
stand in rows on well-trimmed turf:
their neat white stems and arms
present a perfect symmetry.
There lie men who lived in disarray
and died a wild chaotic death.

—GK, 1981

Selected

He heard the jug rattle
the cold coin in the rough clayed
beer jug
shaken in the trench
and knew that this was his moment
wrenched
wrenching his focus forward
to the deed as

The coin slipped out,
head, tail
small nickel,
coppered on the grail
a passing moment's hope
denied
towards escape
from the need
to drag back the man who'd died
from the nowhere land.

Yet the head won

and his head was lost

crossing the wire, the mission
a commission won
not by heart

but because he was entitled to do his part
bringing back the death of battle

dragging him home, pulling the flesh, the bone,
his friend, his friend,
back to safety

Something that either my grandfather talked about, or was written elsewhere. Somme, 1916.

—RH

and he heard the jug rattle, in the struggle

the fall of the coin
wanted, not wanted,

quiet against the coming battle,
the after battle and he

laid there:
iron shot;
the consequence of the fall

of the coin, tossed among the other friends
the shaking jug

all ending with a grin. A tear. A cry.

His loss, his loss, to win.

And fear.

—RH July, 2009

Freedom

Fire devours the jungled slopes,
the desert is pocked with metal rain
and through the choking dust,
the charred forest,
we, the soldiers, come,
bemused, arrogant, cruel, miserable,
ignorant of reason.

'Why do we fight?'

The word is 'Freedom!'

We do not really know
what 'freedom' means
but it sounds a good thing:
noble, fine, worth killing for.

Those Greeks and Trojans,
those Romans and Cartheginians,
those many many others that followed:
they fought for plunder. Riches, land
and power.
How base,
how trivial their cause.
Better to destroy people
for a higher motive.

Better to kill and maim
for something
none of us really understands.

—GK

Displacement Activity

Trônes Wood

Mercy

Clay

I wonder how it felt,
When he knelt, that day;
Was it nineteen sixteen? I know it was the Somme,
Watching the wood.
Trônes Wood.
Life would begin here.

There were no trenches. They were exposed.
One hundred men of the Kents trapped and dying:
The Royal Sussex (the kneeling men) going in to save them.
Into the wood.

What was it like? The wood, I mean.
Shredded, sharpened by gunfire.
No leaf, I suppose, just the jagged teeth of earth, standing
    tall,
Stripped bare,
Hardly covering even the roots that held them fast.

He knelt, held fast. He had no choice.

How did he hold his bowels in place? What did his heart
    say?
The man next to him was a Dead Man. Did he know this?
The Dead Man would save his life.
This much we know: it's almost all we know.
Small knowledge from a time when a wood in France was
    hell.

Trônes Wood.

Here are the shells. There the earth coming up in clouds
    and sprays
And patterns of dark and green and red.
Oh yes, these shells have found a man-mark.
A head rises and falls. Shit happens.

There are men in that wood, lost and trapped.
Clatter, rattle, scatter, gun on tree, gun on man, and the sky
    is splinter-raining.
Move forward!
(Did a whistle blow? What was the signal? I can never
    know. He didn't tell me.)
Move forward!

'It was raining bark and twigs and bits of tree.
Nature came down on us, like a storm. Sometimes, a piece
    of metal took away a face.
It was a dreadful place,
We moved on.
Bleak the wood, not much cover.
Hug a small stump, treat it like a lover. Check the gun.
    Listen to the rain.
Wooden rain, falling on you,
No pain, just shards.
Life shards.

Kents. Poor buggers! Trapped. Got to get on. Got a job
    to do.
Who's firing those fucking shells?
Christ, it's our own side. They're falling short.'

Boom bloody boom. See the earth rise. Why does it take so
    long to rise, so beautiful, that mud, that clay?
Falling away.

Clay time.
I use the time to find new cover.

Rattle. Rattle. Hiss and blow. Scream and silence, soft and
    gentle the flow and spurt of blood.
A dead man next to me, shattered, half scattered. Do brains
    always taste this way?
The taste of shit I know.
Spit!

The Dead Man, though. Hugging a tree.
Watching me. As if he knows . . .
What? What does he know?
(This comes later.)

'Mercy will save you.'
What does he mean by that?

Mercy? No fucking 'mercy' here.
Why does he give me that look?
Oh Christ, here we go again, called forward.

The Kents are dead. Gun fire is now so close it sings. It
    makes the air warm.
It shatters lives, it shatters trees. The rain falls wooden.
Nature scoured by hate, creating a fall of beauty in the face
    of fear.

We lie down and let the soft fall stroke us.
Metal bites breast and brain. Some of us seem to be
    absolved.
Shells fall, shells raise the earth.
A shell falls:

He's drowning.
If he heard it coming, he had no chance to think, to make
    decisions,
To act with precision.
To hold his balls, his rifle,
To fucking run away.
The shell got him. My grandfather, Douglas Ells.
Buried in clay.

So there he is:

'I'm drowning, drowning. Oh Christ, Oh Christ, Oh Christ.
Can't breathe. Can't breathe.
Dark. No air. Fuck!
Oh God, it hurts, Where is the air?
I'm crushed. Dark! Dark!
Stones scratching my eyes. I can't blink. Pain!
Dark.
I dare not swallow. A field of mud is in my throat. This is
    the taste of birth?
Help me!'

Dying, dying,
My grandfather, consumed in clay, clay-choked,
But a man as yet unseeded in the forceful flow of life.
The blast has blasted out his teeth, inwards.

He starts to choke on his own ivory.

Who was the Dead Man?
Where was he when the shell hit?
Was he blown leftwards, rightwards, upwards,
    downwards?
What happened to the Dead Man when he stood
And saw the small, living part of you, my ancestor,
    swallowed by clay and wood, but still in a small way
Signifying vitality.
(Your feet were twitching.)

What happened in his heart? There in the rage.
Where did the courage come from, there in the face of the
    force of death
From which most men would run?

A shovel!

Doug is dug out. The Dead Man holds fast in the storm of
    metal rain.

Digs. Doug.

Dug out.

You lived. And the Dead Man lived. And the Dead Man's
sister was called 'Mercy'.

Mercy Dedman. His sister. My grandmother. You found her
five years later.

I live because of courage and the taste of clay.

—RH, 2007

Love

Shield Man (A Love Promise)

A Saxonian-Humanist love promise.

—*RH*

For all my weaknesses
   despite all that is shallow in me
for all of me that clings to the lost time
   the youth time,
the wildness of the race,

I will be your shield.

And I will stand between you and harm
   in the only time that matters:
the heart time: now.
   The love embrace.

And I will shield the children
   from harm.
The children of your sisters. And of my brothers.
   And of my friends.
And I will never fail in the task
   of standing at
the front, and taking the
   first blow.

And if I fall, I will not have failed,
I will have fallen fairly, and with love.

I am your shield
   for as long as the wood and leather lasts,
and can be held
   on this strong arm—

While I stand
   None will ever do you harm.

—*RH*

Υou

For Annette on our
Golden Wedding
Anniversary

—GK

You are my salt lick
when I am low.
You are pepper in my blood
when we make love.

You are ginger in my gait
when I am eager,
saffron in my soul
on dreary days.

You are
the lavender that lulls
a murky memory.

You are the syrup
that sweetens disappointments:
the gin in my tonic
when toasting success.

You are the aromatic rush
of morning coffee:
the cocoa tide that
carries me into sleep.

You are
nutmeg sprinkled
on my dreams.

—GK, 2011

Thorns

The hawthorns knit across my path
and rake my legs, and yet my hound
runs through their net without a scratch—
this is the way with bold and cautious movers.
A belt of thorns shrinks tighter
round my eyes, as I walk on,
remembering her long manicured fingernails
accidentally catching in my coat,
scoring my chest and cheeks
with careless strokes.

—*GK, 1968*

When She's Away

When she's away
I do not stray, I stay
Waked up, alert
Delighting in all the silence of the night.

And then the chorus.

They sing; by god they sing!
Nothing I have heard, from
Jagger to the absurdity of punk,
No church bells ringing,
Can match the dawn song.

If I break the bed habit,
if I sleep on couch
If my rhythm, broken, hurts my back,
And I crouch (moaning)
in the dawning

I would not change that aching of the limb
For the early, glowing sun,
the symphony of song, the singing
The erudite, the gorgeous sound
Of what is life

All of life.
No violins, no sins,
music resounding, since time was born.

And not forlorn.

—RH, June 2009

Letter To Lavinia

It was not you, Lavinia, that I loved
but the lilac lanterns glowing perfume
and the magical fox that paused and passed
like a piece of darkness looking for its slot.
No, not you Lavinia. The vague voices in the grass,
the warm inquisitive winds that lifted the leaves
and tenderly explored your hair,
but not you. You were a fragment of the whole:
one of the numberless white sparks above
or glistening chips of quartz below.
Ah yes, Lavinia sweet, I know that you loved only me
but I loved all the agents of the night:
their mysticism and meanderings.
When then did they follow you?
Even the lilac trees is bare.

—GK, 1969

Old Love

It is indecent,
this enduring love.
Such passion
is the property
of the young,
or illicit lovers
whose stolen moments
are lanterns strung
through dark times.
We have not fought
against appalling odds
to possess it.
There have been
no soaring mountains
no vast seas
to conquer.
You are too sweet
for lawful fruit,
too lovely not to be
the spoils of war.
We must pretend
we are unwed
or surely we will
shock the young.

—*GK*

1 Met A Ghost And Knew At Once I Loved Her

What are you doing here? I asked.
She replied: I could ask the same of you.
Though she said it with a frown,
Stepping back a pace.
This is my world. Isn't it? I asked.
Mine, she said. I'm sure of it.
Then we've met at . . . where? The Hinterland?
Yes, she said: The Crossing Place.
There was sadness in her face, tears,
The look that tells you there are fears,
Hidden behind the gaze,
But an engagement that set my heart ablaze.

So beautiful, that girl!
Men know the feeling. The whirl of the glance,
The greeting,
The little dance of eyes, when they check you out,
Leaving you in no doubt
That this Crossing Place is a place of meeting.

But because of those tears?
Perhaps the place of parting.

So now I decide. Shall I step aside?
Or hold her?

She is from my world of dreams.
Perhaps to her that's me as well.
Two minds, briefly passing.
Crossing over.

'Who is the ghost? Who the host?
Which mind is real, which mind unreal?

Just let me close my eyes,

And for a while—
Be gone in thought.

And perhaps, from the cruel beauty of uncertainty,
Steal a little smile.'

—RH, December 2007

2 O'clock in the morning: a poem on the baryton

She is an instrument with elaborate frets,
    deeply resonant but difficult to play:
there are hidden sympathy strings to find
    while caressing the music from her eyes.

—GK, 1982

Diverging Lines

Outside Paddington two tracks run parallel.
Same-way trains rattle together, marrying strangers.
We formed such a union, you in your natural furs
and I, forgetting my passion with vanishing breeds.
When I looked, there you were, staring,
and we touched with our eyes through separate
smutted windows, filling hollow needs.
Then the lines diverged, to put us asunder.
A marriage of coincidence, we experienced
the whole affair on separate tracks,
much like many others I have known.

—GK

Memory

I am not closed down by lost love.

There is a passion in me, once expressed,
That flew with laughter, ecstasy,
Not so much
The gentle cooing of a dove,
But the ringing sound of singing, emblazed, inflamed;
Bleeding beneath a loving touch.

I do not like this flesh-old distance,
This hollow heart, emptied of dreams
Harsh-beating with old-year's rage.

Come fire, come flame: torch me—
I'll play the game, shed the skin of age!

Yes, I've changed my mind:
Bone strong, blood strong,
Lost love is lost; we hold
To that which now is precious.

Into each other's arms we fold.

—RH

Ballistics

My brain is shattered by these bullets of devotion—
to be loved with such ferocity is worse than being hated.
The heart-hammer patterns the air with sound
as love, love, love blazes from the barrels of her eyes.
'HOLD ME!' comes as a shotgun blast upon my clay defences
and dum-dum 'darlings' smash into my cheeks and chest.
Ever on open ground, crawling wounded towards the wire,
love whines past my ears its hot, red songs—
the word 'Forever' ricochets around my shell-shocked head.

—*GK*

Chameleons

There are men and women
who take on the colour
of new lovers:
their interests, their politics,
their way of life.
They change their lovers
frequently,
turning, ever turning,
but always avoid their
own kind
lest together they pale
to transluscence
in one another's arms.

—*GK*

*L*ove

Your breath is on your skin.

When I kiss your skin
Your breath is life.
The scent of earth, of sleep,
On the bone-cladding of thin tissue
Once issued from the womb, protection then,
Protection now,
And a treasure I will keep.

—*RH*

*P*oem in Middle English for Annette

Undernethe a ympne-tre
Ich sette me doun to bide for thee.
The tre grew on lofte an ful wyd
Thurgh many a wery wintertyde,
An ther ich lay til luf an lyf
Cam oon agane, with thee as wyf.

ympne-tree—tree of hymns
thurgh—through
on lofte—lofty
luf—love
cam—became
oon—one

—*GK*

Imprints

After forty-five years
the shape of your sleeping form
is impressed in mine.
Here, your right hip fits this hollow,
and there, my left knee
locks neatly into the crook
of your right leg:
our bodies fill each other's curves
and spaces.

Now as I lie awake,
while you sleep soundly beside me,
I muse on your thought-prints
meandering across my mind:
ideas, opinions, beliefs—
but further,
those even deeper tracks
your love has left
upon my yielding self.

—GK, 2008

𝒜 Reflection Of Love When A Dream Is Ended

or Love reflection after journey's end and anger at the leaving

There is no reason—
   In the travelling mind there is no season, no station,
No cup of tea!
   It is an endless track. Once on the rails
There is no looking back.

Who can explain the reason for the rage
   When 'FIN' is writ upon that final page?

I only know that you are the fire
   The strength, the laugh that this old boy inspires!
The soft warmth that gives me courage in the deep descent

To worlds unknown,
   For which I have intent.

Without you I'd be spiralling down
   No insight, a writer not! Just a descending clown.

For Sair.
xxR

—RH, September 2008

Inside Her Are Leopards

Inside her are leopards
prowling close to her skin—
they move to her eyes
and stare out suddenly
to stop me gunshot dead,
before entering her hands
to mark me with tribal scars
or stripe my flanks like quarry
in the fullness of the hunt.
Their souls are there too,
red as blood, but cold,
shadowing our understanding
with all the antipathy
of greater cats for men
in the quick, arcing defence
of some hidden vulnerability.
Sometimes, at night, I feel them
tearing the flesh from my sleep
and gorging on my warm complacency
as she talks of tenderness
and the giving of full hearts.

—GK, 1980

How Do I Love Her?

How do I love her?
Let me count the ways.
My love is like a red, red rose,
Though she's noisy when she blows her nose,
And snuffles in her deepest sleep
And scratches me with ice cold feet.

And still I count the ways.

A bath unwashed, toilet unflushed,
Earns me a biting tongue.
The sort of criticism,
I remember from being young.

And I continue to count the ways.

A bed unmade, my clothing scattered,
Hands are on hips
As though it mattered
That I'm a slob.
The look in her eye?
Don't ask me to describe!

And I firm up and count the ways.

I'm now called Slob, the Rob has gone
The eyes are both despairing.

I'm checked for feet, I'm checked for breath
Inspected for what I'm wearing.

And I STILL count the fucking ways.

(How many ways are there, by the way?)

But without her...

Without her kiss,
her arms, her gentle sleep, her
dreaming in my arms, the blue-eyed gaze,
the thought of all the days we've had,
the days to come,
My life would have no meaning.

Which is why I count the ways.

—RH

$\mathcal{P}$risons

On those dark-early evenings
we would sit at the corner table,
candles like white bars between us,
keeping the darkness close around
in a small prison of light.
Sometimes now I still see the flecks
of flame as I hurry by on the outside—
but she went, long ago.
This is a freedom I do not need.

—GK, 1984

Sadness

Sadness
is not
where something is:
nor is it
where something is
not, but
where something
was—

hollows
are places
that held
sea pools
night suns,
convex
curvatures of me,
you.

—GK, 1983

The Lost Ships

It has been too long
since that horizon severed us.

Confused by stars
fresh from the forge
of a Greek god,
I drift through streets of sirens
like a defeated craft from a spent war.

Those old ships
held the sun
trapped beneath their bark
but there is no heat locked
in this lost vessel,
nor even
a pulse of moonlight.

I do not now seek your signal
amongst the shapes that pass,
knowing that distances
are more than straight miles
as both the Trojan and the Greek
discovered in their sealocked years.

Yet, you and I may touch,
have touched again, unknowingly,
in some storm-peopled street—
who knows whether Aeneas
did not brush ships with Ulysses,
lost in the Aegean fog
in straits like these,
each too intent of purpose:
one seeking an old home,
the other, a new?

—GK, 1984

Life & Death

The Passing Of Alpha

In memory of David Biggs 1926-2009

I was not there
when he walked over the hill
and the light of dusk took his shadow.

He paused for a moment
at the top of the road

thinking of his girls

the tall, broad man, the rock
of his family,
moving quietly through
the stillness;
walking down
to a place we can only imagine.

Imagination, image, magic,
root memory,
that is the old boy now.

His shade,
is one more shadow
in a woodland glade
the dreaming place:
his voice, calm memory,
the alpha purr,
a whisper of love,
and when needed,
a sharp note of direction.

At the break and set
when the light is perfect
we will see the tall man on the hill

crossing the border—

and though he faces away from us
as he must
his breath is the wind of life, and still

and still,
and still.

Old wolf.

—RH, *July 2009*

After Rob's Death

Writers both, we used to ring
each other almost daily,
always with apologies
for startling any thoughts
to sudden flight, to be lost
in the mind's wilderness.

Now, as I hunt elusive words,
tracking the unpredictable,
needing to focus completely
on capturing unused phrases,
I'm constantly distracted
by the phone not ringing.

—GK, 2010

*E*pitaphs

John Middleton Murry, Jnr.
(9th May, 1926-31st March, 2002)

Gentleman and gentle man:
prose elegant, paintings fine,
manners gracious, humour great.
Would that these were mine.

Maggie Noach
(18th August, 1949–17th November, 2006)

Full of fire, full of fury,
fighting for her authors—aye,
I would have no other agent.
Would that she were here today.

—*GK*

Dad

What did you want me to do?
What did you expect of me?

How I longed for your respect
Interest in my life

I did all I could to give the
love surge of your life,

Your daughter

(my wife by any serious thought—
the court evaluation is
pure shit, the idiocy
of so-called 'progressive' man)

as much as colour that can colour life

I give and give
All that I could, all that I can

all that I will.

That is my gift to her.

What did you expect of me? Dad, not Dad!

I tried hard, hard

I keep on trying.

Hard.

All that I have I give, until, until
all that will be taken,

will be taken
in the dying.

You brought beauty into my world.
Shard strength.

The girl whirls, she is my constant joy
I wish you could see
My companion from your life-surge

my champion in all things hard, both good and bad.

Trust me. Trust me.

Dad.

—RH

We The Bones

We rural dead have yeomen's dust
for marrow in our hollowed bones,
and strive to rise with every dawn
wanting to work the river and the fields.
Instead, we lie embedded, urge held fast
by the weight of oceans and earths.
No lunar pull or solar swing can raise us,
nor the sweep of tidal reaches right our feet,
We are the bones, excluded from vertical days.
We rustic skeletons are wickerwork men,
graveyard soil in our skulls for brains.
We are the bones who lie in geometrical poses:
obtuse, acute, we make our angular gestures.
We nestle in rioting roots and wild flints,
locked together, hand on foot, tighter than lovers,
knitting pole with pole. We the bones
form lattice frameworks through the globe.

—GK, 1978

Dying

This is my final touch
of an evening's bruised face—
today the last rainbows
braced their coiled strength
against the hemispheres
and amongst the tasteless ashes
of this morning's last awakening
rooks made papery prayers
unfolding their wings.
I can still smell the night
smouldering on beds of stars.
Is this the way to go?—
with senses blazing,
yet leaving no more trace
than transient springs
made only of colour?

—GK, 1979

On Suddenly Being The Oldest Prick In The Jungle

I am Alpha.
I don't yet intend to be Omega.
Old Alpha gone. New Alpha, now. Here I am.
Morning ritual: howl at dawn moon.
Disturb neighbours.
Close those windows! Go back to bed!
(Instruction in firm voice of new Alpha.)
Yes. This is good. Is it?

I am Alpha.
Beta? Forget it.
Delta? A river thing.
Epsilon? Vaguely heard of it.
Apparently many more letters in Greek alphabet than
Alpha knows
But ALPHA!
He all that matters.

I am he. He is me. Howl at the moon.

And I will remember:

That I was not there
when he walked over the hill
and the light of dusk took his shadow
and he paused for a moment
at the top of the road

thinking of his girls

the tall, broad man, the rock
of his family,
moving quietly through
the stillness;
walking down

to a place we can only imagine.

Imagination, image, magic,
root memory,
that is the old boy now

His shade,
one more shadow in a woodland glade
the dreaming place:
his voice, calm memory
the alpha purr
a whisper of love, affection, a sharp note sometimes
of direction.

At the break and set
when the light is perfect
we will see the tall man on the hill
crossing the border—

And though he faces away from us
as he must
his breath is the wind of life, and still

and still,
and still.

Old wolf.

For all of us, he will always be walking quietly across the hill.

—RH

The Listener

In my narrow home
I can hear drips and drops
echo through giant caverns,
the slide of sub-earth streams
and the dong of hollow cones
in corridors of stone.
I can hear the gurgle
and gargle
of boiling rock,
the exhalation
of steam and sulphured breath.
I can hear the steady tread
of footsteps on the ground
above my head,
the ring of steel on flint
as sextons dig
the house next door.

—*GK*

Keeping You Trim And Tidy

Rob's description
of tending David
Biggs's grave.

Today, we gave you a haircut.

We sat beside you
   and thought of all you'd done
from a time when your hair was dark
   not yet grey.
Not thinning.

We thinned the grass today;
   it was getting long.

Like you, on the mound above you
  the grass grows strong.

Haircuts will happen, while the scissors are sharp.

Soon you will be settled deeper than sorrow.

Until then, we'll cut the grave grass!

(But only every month—and not tomorrow.)

—RH

66

Stone Hill

The earth was opened.

All of history was there.
The old sea, the drying lake
The long dead forest
All composed in death, in layers
Rising through the ice
The age of cold, beast-hunting, clad in fur
Listening for the sabre purr.

Then the age of slayers
And the cast-off pottery of those bold
enough to have thought it worth
to sail the sea
And cut our precious earth.

The fire is there as well.
Heaven's flames, the soul warriors
Seeking a cloud kingdom.

Th earth is cut. The shroud
Disrupts its perfect preservation.
The layered story of a nation.

One more bone
One more moment of life's death
Added to the silent tide.
The clay-claw surf.

—RH, 2009

𝓕ierce Embers

Fierce embers
cast memory into
eyes watching
from a fire-lorn past
and into
hungry, trilling minds
singing with the fledgemouth,
eager to find
the burning, ignition,
condition
of being in the
furnace of finding.

The life of fire is in the urn
the embers, turned:
spark suddenly.

—*RH, 2009*

Gentle Green

Green Man pondered the earth
and saw
that all that was in the earth
consisted of roots
and that which was above the earth
was the product of shoots
and the sweet berry on the berry branch
was the colour of magic
and the music he could hear was made
from brass
formed and played
by the rose red lips
of practised maids

and the Green Man saw
that all that was truly free was on the wing.

And he concluded:

That the earth was a rooty, tooty, fruity, shooty thing.

And with nothing more to observe,
Went back to sleep in the oak-branch curve.

—RH, July 2009

Agrarian Song

Fields of flowering rape
sing yellow hymns
to the sky:
these choral flatlands
carol the coming
of their seed
with strong vocalic colour.

We gather together
choirs of rival hues
on hills that sing
'Hosanna in the highest'—
but the ochre alleluias
drown our rainbow chorus
in a saffron of sound.

—GK, 1981

Fox Dawn

Hunted, always haunt-seeking.
Sleek,
A shadow, silver, moonlit,
Streetwise, street-screeching,
Moonshadow, mercury slipping over walls,
Your calls, cries of fox-lust,
Fox hate
Fox fun.
Silver slivers, twining,
Binding, arms and legs, my street your bed,
My bin your feast;
After the street feast,
The dawn-play of fox fucking.

If men were foxes, (for a while not men)
Would we think of copulating
(With our Vix)
Outside your dens?
And eat the rotten remains of hens,
You'd nicked from nearby coops?
Sneaking up, silver covered against the snow?
(You clever ghosts.)

Probably!
(Don't fancy it, though.)

—RH

My Brother Fox

When the sky turns brittle
and a pale silence is on the land
then shall my brother fox
begin his long winter fast.
He shall come lean from his hill
to seek a feast amongst my fowl,
and failing, find his fellows
to talk of his hollow belly
and the lost summer days:
his stories fanning the coals
of hot red memories
to keep them live behind his eyes.

—*GK*

November Herons

In these grey, heavy days
pressed between blocks
of standing-stone dawns
petrified herons poise
in shallow pools
like pagan priests
ready to sacrifice
the unwilling victim.
Sleek as wet slate,
sharp as splintered gneiss.
Then the sudden
stab, stab, stab,
as their daggers
pierce the hearts
of living silver.

—*GK*

Others

Salute To Boyhood

When I was a boy I—
saw high-flying swallows,
spitting fire across the sky;
drank dandelion and burdock;
sucked sherbet through a liquorice stick;
read the Hotspur, Rover and Magnet;
walked barefoot on cold lino;
wore grey flannel shorts
and itchy socks that never stayed up;
chased girls but didn't know why;
played cowboys and Indians
with a stick for a gun;
warmed pennies in my pocket;
made tin-can-telephones;
loved Cubs and Boy Scouts:
British Bulldog, wide games, gang shows;
ran amuck at birthday parties;
on winter evenings, played knock-down-ginger;
made Guys, sang carols, picked potatoes,
all for pocket money;
formed friendships with gypsies;
built my own bike;
gathered wildflowers for my mother;
took pictures with my Brownie box;
made a pipe-bomb out of Swan Vesta
match heads and iron filings;
blew up the coal shed;
played a penny whistle;
never went a single day
without Marmite and brown sauce;
had powdered egg for breakfast;
charmed old ladies for sweet coupons;
got pinched and punched on the first of the month;
went home with wellies full of water;
brushed my mother's hair for hours on end;

joined the riots of Saturday Morning Pictures:
(Flash Gordon, Lassie, Rin-tin-tin, Roy Rogers,
Tom Mix. Tex Ritter, Gene Autry, Batman).
smoked corrugated-paper cigars;
made balsa-wood gliders that smashed to bits
on their maiden flights;
made stink bombs;
limped to school with one foot in the gutter
and one foot on the curb;
surreptitiously smelled
the hair of the girl in front;
dipped her plaits in my inkwell;
stuffed blotting paper in the inkwells of enemies;
froze in coal-fire classrooms;
learned to whistle shrilly, throw stones,
sword fence with bamboo;
built fires in woods and baked potatoes
pinched from a farmer's field;
made catapults and bought a 0.177 calibre air gun;
hunted rabbits without success;
made box carts with pram wheels;
skinned my knees, broke my leg, caught impetigo;
raced the toilet flush with my pee;
got smutted by steam trains;
hated woollen swimmers that sagged;
went scrumping and got whacked for it;
fished for sticklebacks in a brook;
played board games with a dad
who dented the board if he lost;
made a catswhisker crystal set:
(Dick Barton, Special Agent—Snowy and Jock,
Journey Into Space—Jet Morgan, Lemmy, Mitch and Doc,
The Man In Black read by Valentine Dyall).
played marbles, flicked cigarette cards;
threw rocks up trees for conkers;
kicked a pebble all the way to school;
explored undiscovered continents on my way home;
solved major crimes;
had a stone hot waterbottle shaped like a Maxim gun;

won wars on my own in bed;
darkly and deliciously,
dreamed of girls without their clothes on;
wondered why my sleeping body sinned;
learned to sin myself;
sang lusty hymns at Assembly;
made apple-pie beds for my brothers;
hated school;
bent hundreds of pen nibs on purpose;
got caned;
got hit by flying chalk and blackboard dusters;
ate mashed swede and frogspawn;
took my nan's wireless accumulator
to the charging shop;
laid the tea table to get a halo;
read Just William and Biggles,
Scouting For Boys,
Spick and Span 'glamour' mags
full of naked ladies
(pencilling-in the blanked-out bits),
Rudyard Kipling, HG Wells;
wrote my own stories;
never saw a telly;
felt safe and wanted—
in those years of shimmering winters
and long hot summers.

—GK, 2010

...And All That Was On The Wind

In Memoriam: Natalia Estemirova, Chechnyan human
rights activist. Shot in the head in a foreign forest, July
2009. *And for all the others.*

...and all that was on the wind
was iron
and all that was in the mind was iron
and all that was in the *kinder* was iron
and all that could be found on the blood earth
consisted of raw bone and iron—

and all that the green earth exposed
when the plough horses dragged the shaped earth-scythes
was blood and iron—
and all that the scrabbling, rusting hands,
skin-scored, (tear-stained from the anguish-cry),
could find of what had been taken away
was poetry in iron

and all that the Sun illuminated over the days
the years
was the scattered iron

and all that Gaia rusted, allowed to rust,
in her time-grinding display
of power
was shattered iron

and all that screamed in life's winter
was the scream of what iron had stolen

and yet,
all that suddenly screamed
when the winter had gone

shone with the iron light—
of what iron had not pillaged.

The iron in the heart, the soul,
the haemoglobin, the blood cell, blood pulse, corpuscle
flow in artery, river, holder of breath, breathing—

denied for one, for one denied:

life denial birthing that first, frightened cry,
first look at sky, life won,
the shimmering silver, shining blue:

Iron can never ever take away the colour of iron when it's
true.

—RH

Moon Drunk

One cool evening the moon fell
into my glass of white wine.
I should like to say I tried
to put it back again
where it belonged.

Instead
I hid it with my elbow
and talked
LOUDLY
with my friends
until it had dissolved
into an amber liquid
mellow with lunar promises
of eternal love affaires.

Then I drank it,
quickly.

You see me now
a foolish old man
intoxicated
by a thousand lovesongs,
belching kisses
and sick with sentiment
too rich to hold down.

—GK, 1990

Future

All that I had, I had.
And all that I have, I have.
And all that will come to me will come to me.

When the lady sings, fat or thin
(who's fussy?
I'll try not to be too messy...)
I'll grab her, dance,
To whatever words she chants,
Trying not to swoon;
Give her what she wants;
Take what she gives.
Lovely!
By no means is this 'Last Chance Saloon'.

—RH

Moving

In the Modern Age
we have both gypsy
and settler in our souls.
Wanderlust strikes
as capriciously as love,
seasonal, fitful,
and we answer by
moving house.
Touched by the right hand
of the Romany
and the left hand
of the dweller
we neither roam nor stay:
the house never ripens
to a home
and we walk the same
short stretch of road
again and again.

—GK, 1993

$\mathcal{H}$e Regrets That His Dreams Are Not Fulfilled, Yet Dreams

And in the stars, in the silence of that silent
  world,
Sky-stretched above me as I stretch in sleep,
  Earth pillowed,
The small, much dazzling gleam of eternity,
  the infinity
That embraces the wide-eyed wonderer,
The wanderer in the void of thought;
There, yes there! There is the moment; there the dream.

A little late night madness, under the influence of Yeats, whose anniversary it is!

—RH

I lie on earth. Soon earth will lie on me.
Will I see through chalk, clay; through the finger's dusting
On the wood;
Through the small whisper of parting; the salt drop?

Will I see the trip I need, I wonder,
Find it among those rusting
Fire-rustling echoes of eternity?
Some so old. And some so new. New words.
New worlds of stars,
Where thoughts, like and unlike ours, perhaps begin to
queue,
And radiate,
Hoping to be heard!

Night sky, wrap me round
Hold me in your fire, your future, the memory of fire.
I do not need the sound of fury to be in your embrace,
Only the transport to your echoing, soundless space.

—RH, April 2008

Haikus

March

Hares, hair-trigger legs
and bullet-hard hare-brained heads,
punch holes in the wind.

Poem by a Lonely Youth in London

Comely city girls,
sacred as parkland flowers,
for viewing only.

Freston Wood

Clusters of ransoms
form white clouds amongst bluebells.
I stroll through the sky.

Gambler

The Autumn wind
plays poker, shuffling leaves,
dealing hands of red, gold, brown.

—*GK*

Grass And Daisies

Life and beauty in the City

It's a loud road,
Traffic is a pain—our window box
That small soft scent of
Country rain and sun!

And though we plant with care
All the 'easies' and the 'aises'
All the fragrant names—a
Gardener's delight
We seem to spawn no more than grass
And daisies.

To see them? Morning's made quite bright.
Green, white, the odd bit
Of old red,
Remnants of geranium, or some
Such thing . . .
No tulips, though:
(we'll leave that
to the Dutch).

Our window box is our
Respite. Colour in the city's air.
It parties by night—growing
Calling for the rain and for the sun
A touch of care.

And it always amazes
How strong the grass that grows—
How strong the daisies!

—RH, June 2009

Planetary Raiment

The Earth's overcoat
is woven of water—
flicking through the catalogue
I see it comes in several colours:
sea green, sea blue, sea grey
and others.
The textures of the fabric,
can be variously,
smooth, choppy or stormy,
the latter having many lapels
of white foam that curl away
from its collars.
The hem too, is usually scalloped,
to match any wild shoulder capes.
It is a flamboyant garment,
fashionable among worlds
of this magnitude
and distance from the sun.

—GK, 2011

How The Wind Cannot Change *or* The Wind Was Iron

(1)

The wind was iron
And there was more ice in it
Than in the harsh winter
That had followed him in the hunting.

The wind was iron
And there was more chase in it
Than the gut-clawed desperation
The separation of
Child from the mouth-feed.

The seasons were iron-hardened.
And the new men came.
All changed, except the wind.
All then, was iron
In the time of ice.

(2)

And the seasons were blood-coated,
The wind, iron-hard
The frost soaked in scarlet
The change was
All across the ranging of
The small land
Where the hunt had been all that mattered

All now scattered on

The iron wind.

(3)

And time passed as the sun and the moon
Asked
The simple question
The question,
Always on the iron wind:
Why savage time with
Iron?

(4)

Hard-leathered, hard-armoured, he
Rides into the winter bite of battle.

He has been here before,
He knows
His sons of many generations forward
Will move forward
Against the iron wind.

And that his father had forced his way along the same,
    dread path
And had not been counted in the feast of the raven banquet
The caw-craven despatch of soul and mind and memory
The loss of all. The loss of all.

(5)

So peaceful: that he died so quickly, and
With great brutality,
Hardly noticed
A fact
of no account. One strike
Iron to helm, yet
Who counts the bone strike?
What account
lists the blood drop, the
Brain spill

The limb loss,
The widow left to scour
The killing place
For a trace of what was once inside her
The love inside her
Before the outsider
Took the charm from her arms.
What widow?

Where is the list of
Those who were once so missed?

(6)

And he stepped out of the mind cage, shattering
The bone container
The retainer of myth,
Kept the eyes in sight,
Dragged at the sagging jaw
Blew life into
The incomprehensibility of the fool
Who'd shed the ghost.

'You were my host.
And I belong in you
And I will return to
The savage in your head.
Words and myth made you alive
And made you dead.
The songs that echoed once were full of
Ochre,
The red strip of life on
The rock wall,
The well told tale
The song, the song,
No iron then, just colour
And now just the dolour
Of the iron wind.'
And he stepped back into the mind cage, repaired

The skull,
The dull cranium of man
The sad jawbone, the sad eye
The wasted time
Time wasted
When so much could have been achieved.

But then he began to think
(this creature, this inhabitant
This constant presence in the mind whirl
Guessing at the change).

(7)

Nothing can change man no more than man can change the
wind and the iron wind will always blow and we bow to it
and are frightened by it and the iron wind is in the heart
because that is what the understanding of death has done
to us and what the mourning of a death and the celebration
of that death has done to us and the celebration of birth
and knowing how short that life will be has done to us and
all the knowing and the knowing the span of awareness
and knowing with which we cannot cope because in the
knowing we have created monsters and all that is in the
iron wind is because we do not care because we know we
will soon be

Out of range.

—*RH, July 2009*

Pole World

They once had leaves
and roots that gripped the earth,
but we cut them down with steel.
Now they're returning—stronger,
standing in ones and twos
on street corners: metal, wood
and concrete—standing quietly,
almost unnoticed, in our paths.
Slowly they'll increase in number
until men can hide themselves
in petrified forests of poles
and become hunters and hunted again
and be lost to starve and die
in bewildering thickets of signs.

—GK, 1971

I Am The Forgotten Word *or* Remaining: *echo*

I am the forgotten word
> *sound shared, the common dream*

I am comprised of nothing but the forgotten word.
> *embedded still, deep stream, memory*

I am love, desire, I am the hunt, the death tear
> *time-spanned distance, the yard*

I am the spear, the mud-brick wall, the face of life in death
> *the stone-hard cry; the shard*

I am the words, lost now, that remain
> *shard-sound, the agony of beauty fading*

Which once were proud in their speaking.
> *life in the land-shaping, facing the dusk-*
> *shading*

My courage is defined by words, wandering in the neurone void.
> *we are deep; we are chemical; chromosome*

Defined by poets, chatterers, the reciting voices of all
> *who are not lost; we roam; as the word-users*
> *roamed.*

Who gave grace, charm and action
> *through words, our world defined*

To the repeating cycle of our strong-limbed fall.
> *through words, our worlds declined*

All words are me. I am all words.
In the fold and crevice of the grey, the matter,
There, alive, entombed alive, live great tasks, great story,

Great love, a history of love, song-scatter,
Still active in the hunting of the paint-bright prey.
we have never gone away.

—RH, January 2009

Swedish Meatball Paella

From the Qu..
and yet De..
Cookbook

—R..

Fry twelve Swedish meatballs.
Fry risotto rice in olive oil.
Add onion.
Add one sachet paella spice (mostly saffron).
And water (quite a lot).
Insert Swedish meatballs.
Stir around a bit.
Put on The Best of the Who and open Observer.
Forget what you're doing for some time.
Smell burning.
Rush to kitchen and rescue paella just in time!

Allow to rest (flavour incorporation — important)
Continue to play The Best of the Who.
(Dire Straits optional, but do try to avoid Pink Floyd.)
Start to eat aforementioned Swedish Meatball Paella.
Shout very loudly: this is HORRIBLE.

Never do it again.

(Cook's tip: Sweden and Spain have one thing in common:
the first letter of their names. Apart from that, they have
NOTHING in common.)

—RH, September 2009

Supper And Small Beer

Deifying.
Defying height and death.
The sky to be deified with that stone,
Coarse hewn, ragstone,
Lifted by men in rags.
The point? To be the spire.

Aspire as we will, we die.
Defied by the scaffold.
Deified according to our lie, the lie of belief.
We fall, we die
Deifying the cloud cover. The heaven.

Stone hauled high, managed,
Shaped by hands more skilled than yours or mine,
Perhaps divine.
But put into place

By sweat and fear.
After?
Supper and small beer.
And the wife, as ever, insists on saying of grace.

—RH

Rain

A cloud of birds
exploded like a shotgun
blast, into the face
of the morning—
day reeled, wounded,
falling back
and all along the ridges
came the cry:
Where are the shepherds
who used to give warning?

The hills are empty
of sentinels—hunters
sweep through hollow valleys
like sudden storms
and those men who knew
the old ways
are gone.

—*GK, 1976*

The Coarse Grained Kingdom Of Our Minds

The coarse grained kingdom of our minds,
The deserts of lost desire,
The howling place of face and song,
This is where you and I, my friends, belong.
We are the echo of that wind-charged region.
It is from our imagination, from our lust for life long gone,
That we assemble once again
The legion.

—RH

Remembering

The cyclic seasons merge
into a single grey dawn.

Once was a press of warm damp leaves
lining a nest of sighs.

Once, I swam in her rivering limbs,
a hot fox cooling its coat.

We locked pale in wide meadows
rolled flat by sleeping mares
and she was a breath of feathers
on my breast, a passion of wildflowers
in places where the thorns
patterned my skin with berries of blood.

God, how I miss the heat of moist hay
and the arcing of her rainbow body
burying its colours in my earth.

Now
we are the same dust,
shapeless as the wind.

—GK, 1983

The Coming Of Silence

RH in an email to Vivien Biggs:
Watching Harry as often as I can. Trying to understand.
He comes and goes. I will not let him suffer.
Typical 'Leo'! He keeps taking me by surprise;
never willing to give up the ghost.
Still he has good attention when it comes to supper.
I suppose he recognises, in his feline way,
An attentive host.

I am given the task of letting you go away.

The stripes
Of 'almost white', but mostly grey,
The smell of your fur,
The purr,
The lap dance, lap rest, the curl of comfort,
After the street-hard testing:
A wonderful way to end the day.
Heart resting.

You will be an absence!
(And I am given the task of letting you go away.)

In all the time you haunted
This house,
Undaunted by the rage and growing age
Of the two who confronted their own lives,
Feeding you,
On packet stew;
You were confident with all that came with the wild-night
    hunt,
The feline prowl;
Night not safe from you,
Your silent scowl.

Birds unseeing, then eaten.
And you were a cat, unbeaten
In the night scavenge!
Before the break of day.

(And I have been given the task of letting you go away.)

I will always see the twist and turn of your flanks, that
  clever yawn,
The waiting posture on the grass-greened lawn,
Tail down, limbs ready for the strike.
The leap of faith, in feline eyes.
The kill, wild hunt; the skull death of the finch, the taking
  of the shrike.
The leap into space, sudden and astonishing in its way,
A leap so high.
Bringing down your prey.

And I am not content,
Not at all!
To be given the task of taking you to the end of days.
But: who am I to tarry?
You are not family, you are just a pet.
And yet: my love and I walk to your end of days with great
  regret.

Hard is the loss.
There is no form, no licence
That can service and soften,
The unwelcome sound, soon to come: that hollow sound of
  silence.

Dear Harry.

—RH, November 2008

Kate

They say that her heart
is as hard as stone,
but a plums have kernels
just as unyielding,
yet are sweet on the tongue.

They speak of the claws
of half-shadow tigers,
but tigers lay with tigers
and walk away unscathed.

They say she is cold,
those whose hands
cannot melt ice.

They say she's too distant,
those who fear travel.

—GK, 1979

In His Eyes

In his eyes there was
all that needed to be said
how death would take
the rose cheeked boy
and send him sleeping
the sudden sleep
to earth's quiet bed.

—*RH, July 2009*

Into That Same Dust

Into that same dust
Walking into that same dust
There is the boy.

Gil Gaa Mesh walked here
into the cedar forest
Unfearing. In an older time.

Into the dust
the rose cheeked boy walks
into the dust

all canteen talk
all joke abandoned
nothing matters

anticipation of only the limb shatter
the canvas sack
as the poison in its phosphorescence
blows away the

dust, the boy, life's effervescence

As he walks into the dust
Does not come back.

—RH, August 2009

I Love Life

I love life.
Truly! I do!
I love the stink of it.
I love the sound of it.
And thanks to my glasses,
I love the sight of it.
To coin a word,
I love its 'immenses';
Perhaps I mean its *immensibility*.
And from when I became aware of the possibility,
(When I was much younger)
I still love the taste of it.
The touch of it.
And I want more.

Dammit!
I've just run out of senses.
Or sensibility?

Five of the buggers is not enough,
For an old hound still running in the rough.

—*RH, July 2009*

Mediterranean Yacht Race

Soon all are back and past the buoy,
except for one they fear is lost.
Yet early on the morning after,
just when the winner's glory fades to sleep,
singing to jolly along his crew,
a Sunday Ulysses comes limping home,
mellow with wine-warmed memories
of a night in Syracuse.

—*GK*

$\mathcal{L}$ife Losing

I love the dark. It inhabits me.
I love the light. I laugh there.
I am part of both.
My cloth
is cut from all that has gone and all that will be.
Time is my friend
no enemy.
It holds my hand
Reminds me I'm a man,
Walking
Talking, yes talking, with all my might.
Staring up and laughing with the light.

—RH

Ancestors

Grandad,
a farm worker,
folded fields with a plough.
Dug a trench in France:
it folded over him.

Nanna,
a washerwoman,
took in dirty clothes to boil,
scrubbed herself away
to almost nothing.

Grandpa,
a trawlerman,
broke the sea with his boat.
Met a wild storm:
waves broke over him.

Grandma,
a fishwife,
gutted the ocean's bounty,
went through three husbands,
outlasted the last.

Two of each I had,
and each of them had two.
They stretch back into serfdom.
Toil was all they knew.

They farmed the land,
they fished the sea,
and now their blood,
it burns in me.

—GK, 2009

*L*iving Memory

What are we but the living memory of memory?
We are nothing but the echo of echo;
We would not be here save for
Memory and echo.
The knife that cuts the cow's throat
Cuts us now,
Flesh into meat;
Worm treat,
And yet, when Worm is done with us
We'll leave a book or two, and a fuss,
Will be made of it,
Discussed
In a 'New Writers" Meet.

—*RH, 2008*

Yep. In a go
mood today. N
miserabalissim

—*RI*

Birthday Presents

I ponder on what became
of the gold given to the infant godchild
at his birth.
The frankincense and myrrh of course
has long since evaporated.
But gold is gold,
solid, lasting, heavy with value.
Perhaps it made an Episcopal mitre,
altar chalice, thurible chain, sunshaped monstrance?
No, too contrived.
Or—listen—a christening gift,
for one who later became a pope?
Much too contrived.
Was it sliced into coin, or
crafted into frivolous jewellery?
Not inspiring enough.
Is there—oh could there be—a golden *ring?*
A wondrous ring which brings the wearer immunity
against disease—and even death?
What hope to treasure-seekers and lovers
of fantastic tales!

My final theory is a simpler view:
the boychild lobbed this lump of Mammon's ore,
somewhere irretrievable—
into the dark-green deeps
or down some soundless chasm—
flung it in a state of mild guilt
the way of most unwanted gifts:
hideous neckties, plaid socks,
revolving pencils—
things without soul.

—GK, 2005

Body Language

When an eagle vaults the sky
or inventive Man spears deep space
at superhuman speed,
or a seed bursts like a bomb
and expands,
God is talking
with his hands.

—GK, 1974

*L*og Of Ages

The dead tree stands alone
  limb shattered, forlorn,
all leaves gone, sap taken,
  but beautiful in its death,
in the paddock where young
  unharnessed horses graze.

  The trunk is strong; to
punch it hurts the fist and fingers.
  It lingers on through winter mist
and summer glaze.
  When the paddock is snow comforted,
silent, shivering in the white bleak,
  the shadows of the old village can be seen,
forgotten houses; a shadow roadway in between.

What holds it there?
  What root magic makes this death so striking
in dawnlight and at dusk?
  Age-corrupted, gnawed and flawed.
Heady with mycelium musk.

At Easter, we hide our little treasures
  in its broken bark, in the tree-rind.
Secrets in chocolate,
  memories for future time, hidden in the bole,
for our own little treasures to find,
  following the clueful play of rhyme.

I sit in its shadow often,
  When I visit,
And vision in that quiet place comes easily.
  As the hazed-sun rises, quiet ghosts surface
to crystal-jewel the mottled field of blades.

The dead tree was in the paddock behind Abbey Thorn Cottage – Sarah's parents' house in Oxfordshire.

—RH

The creak and crack of warming wood
is life still; still life.

You inspire me, old log.
    Stay there, and watch the moon-crazed horses,
their wild, unfettered gallop, earth ravage,
    the dawn play, the dusk swerve,
hooves embracing turf, and echo of the present
    sent back to the past-dreaming of the coffined village.

Stay there, and hold against the storm.
    It's a persistence you deserve.

—RH, October 2008

Clerihew on William Penn

William Penn a weapon wore,
quite against the Quaker law.
George Fox however, struck a chord,
with 'Penn is mightier than the sword'.

—GK

Cartography

There are maps in my mind,
old, worn and mellow,
of childhood wanderings
through fields, woods, backyards,
along riverbanks, seashores,
down lanes of white sheets,
over pillowlands, blanketlands,
into dreamplaces.
Newer maps too, of middle age
trampings, seeking work
along hard barren streets,
past long lines of closed doors.
And now these maps
that come with old age,
perplexing, confusing,
leading down blind alleys:
maps leading to word-treasures
buried somewhere,
(where, oh, where?)
oh somewhere surely,
deep in my brain.

—GK, 2009.

Marking The Sky

For CWS
from RH

The cabin stands on a land ancient,
Where once the newly born
Were taken to the river,
Shivering in their father's hands.

Outlooking, the hill has seen the passing of shadow.
Earth-strong, it has absorbed the blood of arrow,
The passing of nations.
The contempt of conflicting stations.

The cabin is the new home. All roads
Once arrived in Rome.
Roaming is ended here.
This is the hill, the river, and the good strong wood
Where love holds dear.

In the hard-carved grain,
Memory of past love is a remaining voice,
Gone without choice,
Wind-taken, not forsaken,
The precious jewel of life,
Carved with soft cuts in the wood
With the carpenter knife.

CWS is Dr. C.W.
Sullivan III, alias
'Chip' Sullivan,
whom Rob often
referred to as his
(American) 'brother'.

Song of past and song of present
Sound with harmony along the river's crescent,
As it curls.
Hill-hidden, forested, white-watered;
All the fears and challenges,
The swirl with the new, the life-embracing girl,
The future as a pole of totems,
The blank on the wood to be carved, as it rises high;
And life so strong that, yes, it can take its
Shaping knife:

And mark the sky.

—*RH, December 2008*

Sometimes My Backside Hurts

Sometimes my backside hurts.
But who cares about that?
Let's talk about my cat.

Bloody animal, always on your lap,
Eating, staring at you, sitting in front of its tray,
As if to say,
'Don't go away. I'll sit here for the whole bloody day!
Staring at the food bowl
Until it's filled.'

Nightfall: damned cat again.
'Can I join in?'
Presses against you, angles itself, stretches legs
('Move over, make room.
Start yielding;
The Cat has returned to the building. Were you not
　　aware?')
Why am I on the floor? Why is my beloved half out of bed?
Why is that cat occupying four feet of mattress? Including
　　where I lay my head?

Life actually is a joy,
As we get older
And the kids get bolder.
Reminders of our half-thought-thoughts, young-thinking,
Half fought, a yearning, not quite understood,
Sometimes won, sometimes lost,
But the cost? Nothing but learning.

And how we yearn to know more, and how much we're
　　taught
By these educated little darlings, full of fresh growth:

They can tell us the exact number of starlings

That can feed and live on a pound of rice,
But also their feather-colour, migrations,
The other countries where they nest, resting
Where strife and inhumanity, by gun and knife,
Cuts through what should be the gentleness of life.

No Chance.
Remember France?

They say that there is music in the spheres,
For which think Planets!
But on Earth we feed on mindlessness and death,
Gannets on fish,
Human life a dish of dead, decaying ignorance.

Once upon a time the stars were in our reach.
Now we are just bones of long-lost hope, washed up on a
    beach.

Unless, of course, we turn our thoughts forward to an adult
    truth,
Not lingering on a childish, bible-thumping youth.

Yes, sometimes my backside hurts,
But in the words of Mr Kurtz:
The horror, the horror!
Is in the hands of,
(To banish if they can) the youngsters of tomorrow.

—RH

Closure

Closure is a myth.
Try to imprison grief,
and it breaks down doors,
tears down bars,
to get at the heart.
In the dreamless night
it wafts through keyholes
to smother else-thoughts.
Powerful and insidious,
it crushes your spirit
or drowns it, slowly.
You can't lock out grief,
keep clear of its claws,
stay safe from its savagery.
Closure isn't an end to suffering,
merely a kink in the line.

—*GK*

Striding . . .

Gil-gaam Esh
Walked out of the mind cave
Pushing aside the Cedar
Tore down the great forest
Heroic in his deed-making
Walked into the future.
He was a man of nowhere
Described by words
On sun baked clay
Lapis lazuli the colour
of his clothes, beneath the cloak
of the hand cured skin
Shoulder broadened by strength, dreams
The great king
Half man—half of the blood earth
Half of the world of dream
The ringing of his story
The blood of his glory
A Time addition to the constant contrition of

My son has died.
My son was killed.
Iron took him
The wind took him.

Myth is beautiful, but
Embedded in the word grave
Between Euphrates and Tigris
Where what was born, in dream,
To be remembered,
Is now a place where
Sons once kissed
are missed.

Are mist.

—RH, July 2009

Cold

The faces of the men are blind today,
their hands buried deep in their hips.
Overhead, skies are frozen still
as a shot of the Crab Nebula
and underneath thick soles
old leaves splinter like thin glass.
Today the blood shuffles to the heart
in crystals: legs and arms are unwieldy
blocks that hang from hooks.
On days like this even the numb note
of the church bell is slow to thaw.
On days like this the frosted owl
considers immortality a threat.

—GK, 1978

$\mathcal{A}$ Ghost On The Road Of Silk

A Peot misses his woman *or* **On seeing the mummies of Urumchi / Love reflection**

Such is the nature of time
That in the wilderness of cold,
The wind grain, corrupted rock:
The sand sea;
Still we can see the beauty of life
Lost but treasured.
Life sublime.

Sand and a shallow grave
Full coloured face
Rich-robed, the heat of life in death,
Laid, kiss covered,
Remembered from an older day,
You look at me.

I walk within the shadow of my dreams.
Light flows.
Who knows what tusk and tooth
Chewed the land you tread?
Who knows what bone-ghost will emerge
From the step, the walk, the track,
Trodden once with firmness, now with insecurity.

A past in colour, myth and poetry
To surface, through your eyes, keen and clear:
An old story, refreshed, renewed: eventually.

—*RH, November 2008*

Fig Tree Bay

(Cyprus)

Here
pomegranate bushes
bleed their blooms,
and olive trees
grow mangled
from the earth.
The sea
is white with scars
and rocks are
blind and cipherless.
These wounds
typify
the body general.

—*GK, 1972*

$\mathcal{A}$ Secret Musician Confesses

My wife thinks I'm living for *'Mañana'*
And that I've gone 'bananas'
Just because I conduct the music
on CD
Of Chopin, Gluck, Bach and Wagner
With a fair-trade banana!
(Late at night,
slightly sozzled.)
I reassure her, when I'm able,
That I'm more than capable
Of conducting Chopin, Gluck, Bach and Wagner
With any available and seasonable vegetable,
Though prices being what they are today,
I must regret,
I tend to conduct (but certainly in a vigorous way)
Chopin, Gluck, Bach and Wagner,
Using a 'passed-its-sell-by-date' courgette.

Couldn't think of a rhyme for 'sozzled'.

—RH

—RH, May 2008

Fordwells

The cold hammer of the morning strikes
the anvil hill, rings out over the valley.
Chisels of ice have carved this hollow
where we live, streams incised its soil:
here, the freezing winds have sawn the hedges:
shorn the trees of leaves. Winter's tools
have wrought such changes in the scape
as they do in me—I am weathered
into new dimensions; shaped, reworked
until I blend into the beaten land,
a rough-hewn figure against the aged knoll,
fitting its ancient stones, its antique earth.

—GK, 1983

All That Was In The Mind Was In The Word

All that was in the mind was in the word
And all that was in the word was in the mind
and all that was in the word-mind
was in the mind-word

and this is getting absurd.

So I'll stop now.

*To Bobbie
Lamming*

—RH, July 2009.

The Owners

The robin that owns the front garden
allows me to dig there, though not without
constant supervision. And while I may
keep the vegetables, any meat is his.
The thrush that rules the roof
reminds me with her twilight songs
that my place is below hers,
though I am allowed to borrow
the use of her perch for my television
signal. The mouse behind the wainscot
tolerates my company, so long
as I remain on my side of the wall.
And the martins in the eaves,
the pigeons in the loft, the bats
in the attic, are all generously prepared
to permit my presence. I am not ungrateful
for this conditional kindness,
and creep about, softly, so as not
to give cause for complaint.
Only the cat asserts her authority,
insistent that I lock myself indoors
when she goes out for the night.

—*GK,1996*

There Is Now An Old Man Of Sixty

There is now an old man of sixty,
Who was anything else but thrifty.
He doesn't smoke, but enjoys a joke,
Let's not discuss the viagorous poke,
Loves the company of chucklin' folk!
And nowhere near broke, yet crunched by the crash
He continues to jig, and to dance and to thrash
To the pagan drums and the pagan dreams
Which mean more to him than it often seems,
As he dances and prances and makes light of life,
And at night lies and stares at his calm, lovely wife.
As she sleeps and she sleeps,
And he kisses that sleep,
Hoping to draw, from that sleep, some of strife.
Knowing that this is the best of their life.
That underaged man of sixty.

—RH, 2008

Fossil

Among the roots of prehistoric hills
I found an ancient scream stamped in the rock:
a fossil of fear in bas-relief, with hideous
face and hanging jaw. It flung at me
those terrors of an age unknown to men.

—GK, 1982.

Frog Assesses His Future

All that was known in the lily pond
Was known to Frog,
from lily pad to water boatmen,
the skimming things
floating.

And Frog sat on the lily pad
and ate all the water boatmen.
Gulping them down, one by one,
no need for goring.

And then there was silence

And Frog saw that to be Frog

Was very boring.

—RH

*F*amiliar Country

We stop
unscheduled
between stations.
Although night
has painted
the windows black
I know this is not
my country.

Outside,
I sense desolation:
hanged men
on windlass boughs
swimming like turtles,
strange birds
weighing the clouds
with wingtip scales
and demons buffeting
against the wind.

We shunt forward,
moving smoothly
down the track
for several miles.
Windows remain
dark mirrors
but the dread
has drained away
as I sense
we are back
in familiar country.

—*GK*

And Time Closed Down

And time closed down
bringing her day by day
closer to the great hooray
that marks either the quiet time or the new time.

She danced and laughed.
She dismissed time
Bellowed that time was daft
Sent it away, to play
with the blood-slipped infants
in their womb juice
As yet no use
and time faced the weaned nonsense
the twisting jumping childer
the *kinder*
and the sulking adolescents
encrusted by the self absorption
of their own half baked excrescence
waiting for the man time,
and the woman moment

when lives like theirs, like the spawning woman
who approaching the change time,
would address affairs of matter
be a monument to life.

Like frog.

Frog sat in his pond, then crawled onto the lily pad,
Ribetting away
Rivetted by the frog thought
that often occupies a frog:
And thought in its frog way
(ribetting)
of the change time.

Coming to Pat.

Alas, had little to add to the discussion.

So that is that.

—RH, July 2010.

Goth

—an unwanted victim
in an age of dull reason
I study pallid lips
for the hint of fangs.
I stroll dark alleys
seeking scares
from sudden cats
or an owl crossing the moon:
born sacrifice for monsters,
willing fate with welcome fears
—such terror is special.
I bare my neck to startled strangers
and plead with pale ladies
for the kiss of living death.

—an unwanted victim,
miserable with all but black and blood,
the swish of theatre cloaks,
the envied shrieks
of graveyard rats
with weasels at their throats
I move happiest in subway mists
and turn in hope at the vampire hiss
of tube train doors
—my swollen heart pumps red
walking through gardens of the dead.

—GK

Butterfly Wings

How quick the wing,
How fast the thought goes by;
Hold it hard, hold it in the mind—
Soon, soon, it will be goodbye.

How quick the wing, the thought, that something,
   It might mean beauty
   It might mean nothing.
Who, with their fleeting
Quicksilver opinions
Can opine about the dream that
Gull-like, floated by.
One more paid-for column among the minions.

We dream on.
We dream of things and 'things', and places,
Thoughts hard earned,
Worlds much yearned,
Some lost, some yet to come,
All in the music of the ring, Imagined faces.

We sleep and eat and live
   On these fragile
   Colourful
   Striking!
   Butterfly wings.
And if we do not hold them fast
They will not last.

Time tells tales,
This flash of life, this living,
This birth of new worlds, this growth of life,
This constancy of connection
Between the ages,
The love, the loss, the laughter, rage,

Always leads to another page.
Another's page of dreams,
A page of 'things', some hard to say, some said with ease.
Floating, beautiful; yet passing.
A moment's tiny breeze.
Butterfly wings.

—*RH*

How To Make A Black Cat

To create a black cat
that in an instant wakes
to a single snick of menace
amongst a concert of common sounds,
whose claws flash out from hidden springs,
whose eyes are swift to cover
every angle of attack,
take a sheet of carbon paper
crumple it, shiny-side-out,
and spend ten million years
breathing life into its breast.

—GK, 2008.

Doubt

Is this the moment then?
The closing down?
The shadow-stroke
That puts the cover on the telescope?
The blind pulls down
Cutting out the light of mind.

I have walked at the extremes of Time.
Now Time has taken away my scope to see
Those breathtaking moments,
Deep past, deep future,
The start and end of mysterious, unknowable infinity.

—RH

*I*ncongruities

Sitting in the sunlight
eating my apple
I am aware that someone
somewhere in the world
is being tortured
by a sadist
with a pair of pliers.

While I lay my head
down on my the pillow
of my soft bed,
somewhere, someone's legs
are being ripped away
from his body
by a bomb.

A child died just a moment ago
from lack of water.
A woman is raped
for walking where she should.
A thousand innocent people
are slaughtered
while I drink my tea.

When I am dying
someone, somewhere.
will be delivering the milk,
whistling a happy tune,
children will be waking
with the smell of frying bacon
as I suck my final breath.

—GK, 2008

Falling Blossom, Falling Silk

A novel in NuHaiku. *

Radiant light of the street lamp illuminates the face of the dead woman.

The silent street is abundant with shadows.

Windows peer with interest from stone faces in the archaic buildings.

Early morning light illuminates the play of cats and the remnants of food packaging.

The engine haze of the motor vehicle indicates the dawn cleaning of the stone pavements.

Only strands of hair and spots of crimson suggest the night presence of the woman.

The avenue is lined by the abundant pink blossom of cherry trees.

Among the shadows, a small figure seems forlorn.

The patches of rust on the investigating machine testify to its ill health and replacement need.

As the town wakes it is unaware of the disappearance of the woman.

The white birds that circle the avenue are like winter snow with feathered beauty.

Behind the shining glass are eyes that reflect the incident in the night.

Strips of paper on the street are indistinguishable from fallen petals of tamarisk.

The shadow of the man is bent as he gathers the memory of death.

The written lines are executed with beauty despite the sadness of the pen.

Shards of the flying machine burn quietly in the children's park.

Clouds drift like exquisite boats where the air was broken by the woman's fall.

The investigating machine has scanned the paper and interpreted the final words of love.

In a narrow alley, the pilot crouches over the hidden body of the fallen woman.

The silk of his parachute encases the broken remains and shines with tears.

—RH, April 2009

Warning: NuHaiku does not necessarily conform to OldHaiku. Often by many syllables and extra lines.

Could this be the new direction of the novel? Each line to be illustrated in haiku form: colour splash, black outline. Japanese accent essential. Underlying meaning to be extrapolated by reader. This is HaikuLit. You read it here first.

—RH

Labels

I understand
those things I understand
and those I do not
I put in one box
and label them
individually—
Love, Happiness, Death, Life—
and so on.
Over time
the labels fade,
become
unreadable.
No matter,
they are all
in one box
labelled
Things I Do Not Understand.

—GK, 1998

For Cal

Hard in thought,
Hard fighting as he grows,
Firm as he seeks direction,
From the 'mind seed' that knows
That forward thinking matters;
Always aware that there is a sinking of hope,
Askew direction in the world,
Where false thinking, and the closing down of scope,
Again, and yes again, are strangling life, with gun and rope.
He grasps and clasps his brilliance, as best he can,
This young, young man,
Knowing that the youthful illumination of his mind
Will one day help direct a new direction!
For what we call 'mankind'.

—RH

*For Rob's nephew,
Callum Biggs O'May.*

*It's a bit heavy, but
you'll work it out!!
Roberto xx.*

—RH

The Conversation: Unreported Encounter

Roman:
I was not keen
To meet this Nazarine.
But when I saw him, all unkempt, ragged, stinking of abuse
I had him cleaned,
Shaved, cheek and chin, hair clipped, clothed,
Perfumed.
He came into my house.

Welcome to my house.
Thank you.
They say you are a king.
The priests? They'll say anything. They're rogues.
Are you a king?
I smell like one. Thank you for the robes.

He was a lean and hungry man.
There was, in the span of his shoulders,
Something of triumph, something of the workman.
Carpentered.

Rough hewn from cedar.
His flesh would fight the wood on which he soon would hang.
He was strong;
the span of his gaze was strong.
He followed me along the marbled hall to where the meal was laid
Where a young girl laughed and played,
And a gentle song was sung.

Conversation and doubt:

(Roman): Welcome to my house.

I'm welcomed.

And to my table. You've been brutalised, I think.

Oh Yes.

Are you able to sit? Or lie? I can make arrangements.

Food and wine suffices. Thank you. I'm already disengaged
from pain.
More pain to come, I think.

That's up to me. Nazarine: a drink?

Wine, yes. I'd like a little wine.

Why do they call you king?

Aren't we all kings?

Me? A Roman tribune? Far from home? Far from Rome?
If this is how a king is treated
Then I'm defeated, long ago.

This I know.

Are you lost?

Oh yes. At great cost. Lost and lonely. No king.
But you, a Nazarine.
Why do they call you king?

Are we not all kings? We die, we fly, we reach the sky,
the heavens.

The sky is for the birds, not men.

Isn't the sky the kingdom of all,
not just for birds?

Words, my Nazarine. My prisoner. My house guest.

But words are what make kings. And words are what deny
the truth.

Ah! Now we come to it.
More wine?

Thanks. But not too much. Wine makes you bleed,
And when I'm on the wood
I'll need
to keep my strength, my aggression.

That I understand. To shout against oppression!
Deny the greed!

Exactly. To shout the truth.

Truth? What is the truth? What is Truth?

You Romans! Certain in action, so uncertain in thought.
Answer me this: What is not the truth?

What is *not* the truth?
Strange question.
What is not the truth, you ask . . . well:
That which is spoken which is not entitled to its truth.

Then what is the truth of truth?

That which is consistent with the act or feeling that under-
lies the words and action.

So if I say that I'm a king?

You are no king, Nazarine. You know it.

And yet a king is what I act and feel.
Or do I?
<u>*Silence.*</u>
What Time defines me?

146

Whose truth defines me as a king?

Your self obsession. And the priests'.

Nazarine:
Then I am a king by lies.
And yet I feel a king by heart. The sky is mine.
Heart, crucified,
will soar.
Voice, screaming on the wood,
will roar.
Blood, flowing,
will stain Skull Hill.
The kingdom of the birds is mine. The nests of worms are
    mine.
The shattered
ears of men
Undeafened by my rage are mine.
Men who in a king's name will preach as easily as they kill.
That is the kingdom of my death.
That is what is gifted to me.
Whose lie? Whose truth? What truth lies outside—or
within—the cage?

Roman:
We are harrowed by the cage of words.
The lip-speak that beguiles.

More wine?
If it's your last cup, let it overflow.
Everything that's on the board is yours.
Cut meat, cut bread, cut fruit. Feel free.

Stay with me.
Please stay with me.
And talk until the talk is gone.

Gods! How I long to visit the Isles
Where men can think.

Stay long!
Use your knife. The edge is keen.
When we're done,
Nazarine,
I know I will deny you life.

—RH, 2008

Malta

Land of stone and stones, rocks
weighing down the red fields
and slotted into walls—mile
over mile, tier on tier,
snake-eat-tail. Limestone
villages, extensions
of the walls,
with houses fused together.
Formless tawny blocks cut from
rocks with handsaws. Statues:
Joseph, Mary. Stone, damp
with history: caves, stacks,
grottos, temples, combs, cliffs,
even the sea is tideless stone,
sealing the bone and brick and mud
together into cities that sank
back into the soil, and were
found again
and cut
and used for patching walls.

—GK, 1968.

Flight

I am balloon headed
Flying high
Charged with creation
In the wind blast of the sky.

The clear view. The opened eye.

The fall will come,
The shot bird plummet
Into the forest, (though not yet)
Dead dreams at rest,
Nesting,
Back in the clutches of the ordinary nation.

Yes, I know the fall will come,
But I am not possessed by desperation.

Strong will, good humour
The strength of friends,
Will take me—thank you Mr Bowie—

From Station to Station.
Station to Station . . .

—*RH, November 2008*

Balloons

I love to see the skies
full of air balloons,
hanging puff-cheeked,
from breezes:
the people-carrying kind
with gondolas below.
They decorate
the blue backcloth,
with their stripes
and colours,
the passengers
standing stiff with courage
in delicate machines,
handkerchiefs
fluttering goodbyes,
pale faces
shrinking to dots.
I love to see the skies
full of air balloons,
yet fiercely cling
to this fragile globe.

—GK

Stands There Like A Fawn

Stands there like a fawn
New issued from the ruck
Clean licked of mud
As a womb-choked wail washed clean of blood
All guile yet to be time tested
Immune to the furious flood of death.

In the last moment

There is an ocean in his eyes
A deep drawing down
Inviting the sea quest of memory.

The ivy gnarling of his hands
Displays the shape of bone
Clutching the hard and polished wood
Strong in this abating storm;
The quick-song of leaving
Heaving to find the upright
The sky search.

So that once more he stands there
Like a fawn, new issued from the rut
Clean licked of mud
A womb-choked wail washed clean of blood
Embracing breath
All guile yet to be time tested
Immune to life and death.

And its furious flood.

—RH

Robert Holdstock

In a place undreamed
he created a forest.
Books became trees again,
black ink their sap.
Rotting mast, dead moss, dark bones.
Each page pungent.
He filled green glades,
narrow paths, dense thickets
with eldritch beings.
A place where mystery writhed
like smoke behind the eyes of masks.
Where vines of plots
twisted and turned in on themselves.
Fresh fables flourished here,
old legends grew new leaves.
Strange beasts stormed into our heads,
ancient heroes returned
to seek new destinies.
So deeply entwined,
the writer and his work,
that when he left the real
he slipped complete into his otherworld.
See, there on page sixty-one,
there, beside that riot-rooted oak
where shadows break the sun,
the tangle-bearded Rob looks out
and grins at us in fun.

—*GK, 2010*

The Crossing Place

The crossing place is where we meet, and where we part.
The crossing place is where we test our heart.
The crossing place is where we turn and turn:
It is the moment's pause;
The road where we make selection.
Yes, this is the Shaping Place!
Yearning comes strong here.
At the crossing place we find our next direction.

—RH

Cyprus Shepherds

There are some faces
as uncomplicated and rough
as cave-wall frescos;
faces of shepherds
that were never as young
as the minute-old lambs
they wear like scarves;
faces that eternally
rest on ash staves,
hawking and spitting, splitting
scrublands of beard with grins;
sun-burnt, star-burnt faces,
raceless as their work,
shouting the soundless greeting
of men who work alone—
faces that came before a king
before the coming of kings.

—GK, 1969

The Forest Feast

The Green Man slipped out of the blood place
The snake penetrated cave
and came into
the wild
the wilderness where a rave
of impossible dream
watched the dance of clay, still living
not yet in the claw hold
of Raven;
not yet the licking lips of death
the feast of night, dancing,

And the Green Man pushed apart
the strong thighs of the elm
Crossing the crack
hearing the craic
the songtime of delight.
And peered out, glancing,

The feast was straw.
And what a feast!

All that had died was on
the earth plate
Rotting down
shedding the maggot thought
the larval scrunch of life
the marinade sauce of struggle
once intended to
be so Green.

And the Green Man watched as
the feast was scrotched and scarfed.
and all that was once wood
    was chewed

For the
banquet menu
at FantasyCon
2009

and all that was once Spring
   was gulloped
and the summer berry
   was consumed by
belly, thoughtlessly
   as if that ripe fruit
so delicious to the tongue, the mouth,
   would last
beyond the meeting,
   that time when young, when sour,
and in its sea season,
   would make its salty kiss less a reason—
more a pleasure
   For the eating . . .

And the Green Man watched
and knew this.

The woodland kiss
   is the embrace of time itself.
There is no man there
   just the fold of arms
The gentle hold of long forgotten charms.

Feast, Feast!
Whatever beast
is plate-splayed. Feast!
Drink well. Drink deep.
And in the evening—rave!
Let rafters ring!
The Ravens ask no payment to dig our graves.

Before the ravens come, just sing!

—*RH, July 2009*

Snow

During darkness
the world donned a white mask.
The scene is sinister despite
this specious guise of purity.
Streets are cloaked with calico,
houses and cars blindfold.
What has this planet done
that it hides its face? I am fearful.
I wait behind a window,
hoping hourly for tell-tale stains,
but night returns and all stays wrapped
in swathes of moon-pale bands:
a bandit before a pre-dawn raid.

—GK, 1983

The Kettle Is A Drum

For Roy Kettle, Chris Evans and Garry Kilworth.

The Kettle is a drum
Bang it and it makes loud noise
But the Kettle-drum we know
Is civil-servanted, and keeps poise.
When his drum is banged, his smile and swift and cheeky
    glance tells all, that
nothing tarries,
That nothing teasing has him whanged or whacked.
Wisdom and great laughter are in the small, close-
    shouldered pack
He carries.

The Heads of the Valleys shuddered and shrank
When Evans left Tredegar, the valley,
Joining the rally of simple minds in London
Where a grimed street must pass for a stream-filled silence
The flow of old life

He found a wife.

The Heads of the Valleys were uplifted.

Moving on is being strong.
Old Tredegar sings its song.
Evans still sings along.

Essex birthed a man
A strange sea-surge could have taken him away.
One day, in nineteen fifty three.
Now he sees beauty in the mudflats, the drowned shores
The harsh bleak, the curlew cry
of the loneliness of what will soon be eaten by time.

He is the recorder of the time.

All that is gull swoops and is known to him.
All that is winter is harsh and blows through him, and is
   known to him.
All that is sudden in its burst of colour, on wing or petal, is
   known to him.

To the west are the Marches; to the east the marsh.

We cross these places, and grasp hands.
We speak, we laugh, we reason.

That is how it is in this longest, lingering part of the sea
   season.

—RH

Poem For Amelia Rose

Amelia Rose has several toes
(five on each foot, naturally)
just a single nose
(which is right and proper)
and a Posy-like pose.
Amelia Rose
plays sweet concertos
(on her elf's violin)
and knits French bows
(with her knitting thing)
all of which shows
How many talents and toes,
(not forgetting the nose)
are Amelia-Rose.

(And they're all MINE! she said.)

—GK, 2003

Written for the daughter of friends while visiting. Three years later, quite independently without knowledge of this verse, Rob wrote his own poem to Amelia Rose, also while visiting. Clearly this young lady fires the poet.

The Other Tygers

Why is that Tyger burning bright?
And why is he running around on fire (apparently)
In the 'forest of the night'?
In pain. Squawking.
If you're in flames, Tyger, don't hang about! Don't stay.
Jump in a lake, you fool,
And put the darned flames out.
Get cool.
And then go stalking! Prey!

But what about the other Tygers?
Shouldn't they get a look in?
You, Tyger, Tyger,
I'm talking to you!
You of the Forest of the Night—
Ok! You're cool. No problemo.
We know you're bright.

For Amelia Rose: sorry about the rhyming . . . and the word 'darned'.

—RH

But is it right to ignore the other Tygers? Like:
The Tyger of the Forest of the Dawn?
After all, cats yawn, waking up with the rest of us.
Expecting their food to be laid
On a tray,
Like something sacrificial
proffered in front of them!
Fat chance, mate. (I say to my cat.)
Cats don't (to my knowledge)
Eat toast and marmalade!
(Which, at that time of the morning, is all that's being
offered.)

The Tyger of the Forest of the Elevenses?
Tyger tea and biscuits.
Yum yum.

And what about the Tyger of the Forest of the Afternoon
Nap?
Well—
He's probably a writer.
Clever blighter.
Ho hum. But forty winks? A must!
Or the Tyger of the Forest of the Afternoon Tea?
More biscuits, yes, but now they're a tad more chocklateee.
(Managing to rhyme, here. Just.)

The Tyger of the Forest of The Sun Goes down?
The Tyger of the Forest of the Quick Snack Before Supper?
The Tyger of the Forest of 'Just ten more minutes of TV?'
The Tyger of the Forest of NO! Go to bed NOW!
The Tyger of the Forest of the Kiss Goodnight?

And that last and lovely Tyger:
When all that's now required, it seems,
Is the Tyger of The Forest of Good, Happy,
And Creative Dreams.

So many Tygers,
So few rhymes,
Tygers clearly live through difficult times.
But I reckon all those Tygers mentioned are imploring,
'Forget that so-called "Burning Tyger in the Forest of the
    Night!"'
'He's got it made,
'His rent's paid,
'Pension fund to die for, lucky lad,
'Thanks to William Blake (Good Bloke, a little mad)
'Who, though he couldn't make the first verse (of his poem)
    rhyme,
'Has added to our language something quite sublime.
'Something about tigers on fire? In the woods? Did we
mention that?
'But enough of him!

'Pay to us a little more attention!
'The other Tygers! Us! Yes! We're not boring!
(Except for the Tyger of the Forest of the Noon Day Sun.
He's snoring.)'

—*RH, September 2008*

The Arab Ironsmiths

(Bahrain)

I have seen them standing waist-deep in pits,
using the hard earth to anchor their anvils,
working in pairs under a low tin roof.

Their charcoal fires scattered between them,
flaring and dying like stranded comets:
spitting sparks and nursing glowing ingots,

the smiths hammer and turn, hammer and turn,
with an inbred, mystical rhythm and skill
longer than a lifetime takes to learn.

Sawn-off men with sunken coalblack eyes
and sinuous narrow limbs
working with a handful of the earth's core:

beating life and beauty into a rusty harness;
shaping fleur-de-lys hinges for teak trunks
out of old chains and slave manacles,

while the nature of their work
forges their bodies into early antiquity:
humps their backs and grooves their brown faces.

Grinning, legless gnomes in dirty vests
that fashioned the weapons and war trappings
for mighty armies led by kings of kings.

—*GK, 1967*

Vibrancy And Chaos

Vibrancy and chaos shape the change;
The field is wide;
This is where imagination ranges:
The hunt for that forbidden glance, the smile
The sudden twist and turn, the guile,
When a friend becomes a stranger...

And all that you knew is lost
And all that you thought lost
Is new again,
And the cost is only in the changing,
And in the re-engaging
Of the field
Where vibrancy and chaos bow
To imagination!

To the mind they yield.

Sent to Petr Kotrle, Rob's friend and Czech translator.

—RH

The Bull

Old Age is a bull
I once saw raising dust
in the far distance—
too far off to worry me.
When we came closer
it seemed he was
marking time,
waiting for me
to narrow the gap.
But now—now we see each
other clearly—
man and beast,
he turns
and charges me.

—GK, 2008

Trampoline Boy And The Back Flip

For Louis

Louis is Rob's nephew.

The surface on which he dances
      Casts him up
Sends him skywards, towards the cold, but
      Waits for him
And grasps him as he lands again
      A loving hold—
The game is on!

Upwards! His arms sky-reach
      His eyes are closed, his face
A smiling mask of joy
      And down again, to where
The embrace is brief and
      Absorbs the cry of 'more!' and
Throws him up for

One more cloud-clutch
      Hair flying, arms outstretched
Every sinew, every bone
      Every flex and twist in air
Ready for the touch, the tryst
      Between sky-rising boy
And the surface where
      Faith in the acrobatic life is honed.

He hits and rises
      And surprises the eyes of
The watching birds as

He turns on his back
      Only air to grip
Turns back and back again
      The double flip.

Ascends, descends, hardly
Touching surface, embraces space
He belongs here!

No kite nor kestrel
No crow nor finch has
Ever matched the laid-back, air-calm
The lack of flinch
As he rises, turns,
Comes down, stands
So still:
On the edge, but in complete
Control,

And with a grin that
Signifies his future
And a quick glance to his audience

Leaps again—once over—
Onto his feet, onto the lawn,
The final (for the moment)
Perfect roll.

—*RH*

The Narrow Vertical

The
mind
takes
pleasure
in thin
towers:
spires
lancing
the sky;
pinnacles
of gneiss
skewering
the sun;
pines
that
flick flies
from
clouds;
a lean
sky-
scraper
rising
from
the floor
of New
York
to bend
bow-like
in the wind;
minarets
like spears;
tall
slim
rockets
that kick
the globe
goodbye.

—GK, 1969

The Long Drop Upwards

—having vertigo, you lie spreadeagled, face upwards
towards the pit of the sky
envying the safe trees with their roots roped to rocks
and the casual hawks pressing their backs against the wind;
the stone-still bats hanging blind in the caverns
like stalactites
and the mole boring itself to sub-zero heights.

—having vertigo, you wonder, not at the length and breadth,
the span of space,
but how deep? how deep is the fall of the black shaft
of the universe?
and you cling to the flat green meadowgrass
afraid to close your eyes in the case the floor
becomes a ceiling.

—GK, 1975

Stone In Antarctica

A Meteorite's Tale

Black, blackened by fire
You hurtled through the atmosphere.
Landed on ice.
Hard, hardened by time,
Made in a place where time means something different
To this most savage place.
You raced, perhaps with friends,
Through space
Silent product of a dying light.
A world died to make you.
A world received you.
Welcomed you onto the ice.
Your fire cooled. This was the end of days for you.
Stolen from the star that formed you
Given cover, a grave in new ground,
Ice bound, silent, a place that should be left in peace.
Your new world, loud, yet quiet in the mourning wind.

A pebble? In the snow?
You were more than that.
A stone of stars.
Icarus in the void.
You flew from sun to sun.

Your furnaced, flame-fired crash to earth brought
Thought to an understanding
Of beginnings.
Your end was not the end.
My friend, you were at peace upon my southern shore.
Antarctica.

Where there should be no feet stepping,
No ships,
No further hurtling of the wasting life of time,

Money bound, men, women,
Caught in the enamour
Of your beauty.
Ground in desolation.
Nothing to do but kill for a kiss of the camera.

We should leave you in isolation.

Life flares and flames, burns bright
Cools. The fire is taken. Flesh turns to stone.
Antarctica is different.
It should be left alone.

—*RH, March 2008*

Simon Jenkins wrote today...
in the Guardian, essentially
enthusing for tourism in Antarc-
tica, his case being that 'it doesn't
matter because everything is
going pear-shaped and why fuss
about a large piece of ice-covered
rock'. He came home from a
visit there with a small black
rock. A fallen thing. Anyway,
here's my thought on that small
black rock.

—*RH*

The Next Cézanne?

In Provence
on a high village road
I saw a young man.
He was about nine or ten,
flicking the hedgerow idly
with a switch, and staring
thoughtfully at broadly
scrubbed fields that surged
at the base of a burnt-
sienna rockface. In baggy
shorts and shirt soiled
the colour of rust, he was
perhaps the next Cezanne?
Or possibly the next
village baker, cobbler
or mechanic? Infinite
futures were held fast
by that small frame,
those eyes caught suddenly
by the parched colours
flowing from dust and stone:
locked for a moment
in the tidal race
of his own landscape.

—GK, 1984

*T*he Stick Speaks Of Age

The stick speaks of age
But your heart is strong.
May you live life for love.
May your life be long.

—*RH*

Street poem. The parting
words, on meeting an elderly
Caribbean exile, using a
walking stick, who greeted
me with a smile, and with
which, indeed, I greeted him
back. (Not the same smile.
My own.)

—*RH*

What A Strange Thing Is A Brain!

What a strange thing is a brain!
Like a train, entering a station,
Sometimes it arrives too fast; wives,
Wave at disappearing husbands.
Sometimes it grinds to a slow stop.
But either way, out pop
(when the brain-train doors flick open)
Lives.
Good old brain. Doesn't always function.
But always sees new sights
pausing at a junction.

—*RH*

The Silence

We sit in one room,
one-minded, in quietude.
This we call Meeting for Worship
which for me is not so much Adoration
but a mental falling-away
from the world around me,
a drift into calmness,
a shedding of jagged thoughts,
weighty cares, pressing problems.

This is the Silence
adored by Quakers
for being what it is:
one hour of
stillness,
severence from shopping lists,
bills, boilers that break,
dentists and doctors,
Myself.

A time to consider
Concerns:
war and poverty,
unnatural disasters
and other lunacies
at which we chip
hoping to uncover
a saner-shaped world
beneath.

—GK, 2009

Walt Whitman Did It For Me, And Continues To Do It

How did Whitman put it?
Well, sorry to steal, Walt, but here I go:
I dream in my dreams all the dreams
Of the other dreamers.
And I become the other dreamers.

Thanks for that. Beautiful.
Sorry to nick it. But you do impress.
You address my fears, old boy. You long dead
    man
Lost in that Unknown Region
Where, as you yourself might have said:
A legion of a legion's land have moved, migrated, lived and died;
Spied out the rocky cover, to live;
The dove to shoot and eat, to hunt
The strong limbed buffalo
Whose flesh feeds, whose blood warms,
Whose stretched, tanned hide protects against the snow.

What a marvel of a man you must have been,
What education, in the form of insight you must have seen
Into those other worlds.

Thank you for your gift.
Some of us are uplifted by it, some are not.
But you'll last, my friend.
Your end was not the end.

So here's my short, and well-meant take,
On the life on which,
In Unknown Regions, you staked, well,
Everything.

In my dreams I scream.
And I scream all the screams of the other screamers.

Written because
some of his lines ju
bloody inspire me.
Including three, fou
and five below. I
have much quoted
him in my books.

—RH

Dreamers, just like me!
And you (you thoughtful man).

I live a hundred years away.
You've been much the same time in your grave.
I'm trying hard.
Soft life.
You had it harder.
I will take your vision to my bed.
My dying bed.
Even as now I take it to my living bed:
Where I celebrate the visions of a mind that saw the
    Region,
Where I dream of what might have been dreamt by that
    man's mind,
Where I wonder how he imagined the greater world,
Where I envy his experience, and the way he met the
    stranger who had come to settle,
Where he stared at ships and pondered the life that would
    soon be disembarking.
The man who looked east to where these people came
    from,
And respected them.
And to the west, to where there was an unknown game.
That Unknown Region.
The place that would kill;
The place that would fill the hopes of children, or bury
    them.
The place that would either fulfil dreams or dismay them.
The place where new bones would brighten hills,
Hills still scattered with older bones, now corrupted;
The place where hills would shadow new homes, cruel
    stations,
On the graves of old homes, past lives,
Interrupted by the movement of nations.

The place that would silently reveal its secrets.
The wild place, unknown yet known
Unconquered but for a long time conquered.

That was your vision, Sir:
That the Path we walk is not so much about the walking,
It's about the path.
Ever changing.

It would not exist if it had not been forged before
By a thousand soft feet, softly stalking.
Ranging.

Thank you.

You lived in a land, hard and harsh, I know.
I was born on Romney Marsh,
Where a hard, salt-scented wind blows.
And yes, I can smell it now.
What we have in common is the region where strange seeds
    are sown,
Seeds that, for a while until we understand them,
Are unknown, unkissed.
But not to us. We soon see beyond the mist.
We are explorers of memory.
Memory itself is life-bound, time-bound,
Given as a gift to those who know its value.
When we give it up, we drown.

I don't believe in god.
I do believe that time and life,
Evolution, struggle, blind fury,
A billion years of feeding, fucking, goring,
Led to the creation
Of that most wonderful of senses:
Imagination.

And from imagination, after all,
Comes the wonder, the diversity, the colour
(Let's not talk about the dark)
Of nation.

—RH, 2008

Tree Messiah

When trees can talk
they will tell how brutal hands
cut down their tall prophet
from a sentient slope—
they will speak of pagan tools
that scissored away the gold-green arms
from the holy son of the forest
and how the bark-robed trunk was
split and crossed—
they will tell patient judges
how their lord was dragged
through jeering crowds, and crucified
against the body of a man.

—*GK, 1980*

Wind-Shaping

For all the kids!

The wind sends its swirling signal.
       The sand is shifting along the beach
And the playthings are running
       Away from the sudden
Fierceness of the sea
       The shifting tide, the wave-surge
In the sudden, sundark cool.

Where is shelter, now,
       As the sand shatters
And the summer castles shed their grains
       To join the flatness of the
Shadowed strand?

It can be found in the quick-erected
       Canvas shield
In the family huddle,
       In the car-space, or the caff;
The muddle and the skelter
       Of the brief escape from what is real.

And yet, the young one went out
       And crouched upon the strand
And absorbed the wind-howl,
       the crystal whip,
The skin and soul-scouring of
       That change.
No rough sea, summer storm,
       Strand-shattering, play-battering,
Can cause an everlasting mourn.

The dark sky breaks apart.
       The young one starts again

Gathering the strand, shaping it,
    Moistened with a bucket of
Calm salt tear, new tower,
    To stand, a fragment of a dream,
New form on the living shape-shifting shore
    Brightness lifting, the sky promising
No rain as yet, despite the glower.
    For a while, then, the smooth, soft erosion
Is marked again.

—RH, June 2009

Rhubub

Right leg buried somewhere in France,
the rest of him deep in a hill
overlooking the river
where Cnut fought Edmund Ironside,
and brought Dane law to East Anglia.
They called him 'Rhubub',
he being lengthsman and gravedigger,
and so he called
his plodding pony 'Custard'.
A black-haired mongrel named Mick
rode postilion on the cart.
He tended verges between villages
keeping scythe and sickle order,
wearing a greasy cap, collarless shirt
and filthy jacket, the pockets sagging
with pipe and baccy, matches, penknife,
and a thick wad of soiled notes.
Within ten miles he was known to all.
'There goes old Rhubub.'
He was the market square clock,
the stone water trough,
the cobbled cattle pens,
the King's Head:
a monument to those bygone days
that smelled of steaming hay,
sun on sweeping cornfield,
ditch weeds, hedgerow, deserted nests
and an ancient light laying on the river.
He was Rochford.

—GK

Yssobel's Song

On the Death of Arthur

I came to the strong place which I knew I must hold,
I came to a time in my life, and I knew I must hold,
I came to the hill where the harnessed host was waiting
And the wind was waiting
And a storm of rage still silent, waiting.
And I knew that I had to hold on to what I had been given;
And that the world was changing, and that I had to hold;
And everything that I had once been given was gone,
Yet everything I had been newly given was with me.
Under gloom-grey sky, and over red-green earth,
We held and held until we broke.
But in the breaking, we held, and in the holding we will find,
Avilion.

—*RH*

This is a song: Yssobel (my young heroine) has dreamed a song of the death of Arthur, although she doesn't know it's he. All she knows is that the man she dreams will be a part of her life. Her father sees the song as reflecting her own death. I haven't decided on the music, but probably either by Leonard Cohen or Queen, who all appear as mythagos.

—*RH*

Time Flows

Time flows in the Riot of her Blood.
She is sap green and ancient;
Time?
A flood within her veins.
She knows that nothing's lost and nothing's gained
Where only land and sea and river thrive.
We pass like shadow.
Blood will riot briefly, no denying.
Time is used to the sound of laughter and of crying.
But Time alone, and cloud-caught memory,
These vast and transient notions are all that will survive.

—*RH*

The 'Crab' Poems

After Ted Hughes's 'Crow' Poems

Written to celebrate the engage-
ment of my friend C.W. 'Chip'
Sullivan to the wonderful
Sheree; and he told me how he
worked it...

—RH

Sullivan's Crab Soufflé

She would always remember the day
When he romanced her
with Napa Valley Chardonnay,
Followed by his special crab *soufflé*.

Meat so sweet upon the plate
A date that would lead to
A tide-swell of heart-lustre,
From the simple cracking of the shell,
The ocean's egg;

The moment's muster, the summoning
Of kitchen skill

To take life onwards to the hill,
The new horizon,
Orisons of the night talks yet to come.

Crab played his part
In the heart-union.

The new start.

(And yet, and yet:
Whoever thinks of Crab ... ?)

The Birth Of Crab

Crab was born
As sea spawn,
Grew, and soon had claws,
Mighty in the sea-craze,
Terrifying to the forms of
Conger, shark and rays,
(And they went away).
And Crab ruled his rock
Magnificent, in fear of naught.
(Unfortunately, he got caught.)

Crab's Great Task

Crab was called upon
To fight the eel,
The huge slime-beast of the coral,
Stronger than all the other slime-beasts.
And Crab armed himself
Faced the great conger in its cave.
And brave Crab killed the eel, and ate its heart,
Stripped the eel-flesh (ate it also),
And with maddened purpose
Took the eel skin, strong as steel,
And made a cloak triumphant of the scales.

The glory of that deed
Lived long in the sea-tales.

And Crab was revered.

Crab's Mysteries

All that was known in the sea
Was known to Crab.
Claw-waving, Crab was
The greatest of the sea-beasts.
And his understanding
Was greater than the whales'.
Great Crab—silent, dignified—
Understood all that was in the trawl
In the mouth maw
Of the great sea.

Alas, he did not anticipate the stone beating
And Sullivan's *soufflé* eating.

Crab's Last Day

On the sea bed,
Side walking,
The blue so still — the ocean
Quiet:
Crab knows his girl is close—but—
Net grabs Crab!
Crab's girl emerges from her hole.
Her scream is unheard in the ocean toss,
As she wails and grieves
Her rope-weaved loss.

The Death Of Crab

The hammer fell; this was the time
Of the stone smashing
Releasing the soft flesh,
The blood mash.

Crab cried, but no escape
From the stone lashing.

Crab's Forgiveness

Alas, Crab did not forgive.
And the 'Night of the Crabs' saw
The terrible claw-tearing, the life taking,
By crabs ungoverned (by crab law
Which they ignored)
On the isolated homesteads where
Soufflé was in the making.

Crab And The Sea Law

The killing of the slime beast
   The great conger
Did not go down well with
   The eels.
And Crab was summoned.

Crab was facing the
   Sea Law—
The law of Ocean—
   The sea surge of law
(Which does not depend on luck)
   That gave nothing,
In its judgement
   For the brave bite
Or savage claw of
   Such as Crab.

And Crab, it seemed, was
   Well and truly fucked.

But CRAB WAS STRONG!

Crab Goes To Court

Crab played along with all
   The tall, slimy, scale-suited
Beasts—
   Paraded before him, hoping to
Break him,
   To administer the shell smashing.
In the name of the Sea Law—
   The cruel, hard notion
That all, which lives below the waves,
   The silvered heave, the restless tug at land
The call to the drowning-death of life,
   Is ruled by Neptune
And not by Fortune . . .

And Crab had his answer ready.

Crab Defends Himself

'The great conger
   Was considerably stronger
Than the other sea beasts
   Except for the whales
Who do a lot of prancing (and are far bigger than me)
   But the conger is no longer
A danger
   Except for the dancing.'

And Crab rested his case.
(Hoping for laughter. None came.)

(But alas, he hadn't done enough.
Sea Law is bloody tough.)

Crab Pleads Ignorance

Under the sea
  Crab was not tasked
With revising for a GCE.
  And yet Crab was wise.
French? He'd had it—couldn't speak it.
  Russian? Incomprehensible. Even though
He'd tried to tweak it.
  Astronomy? Domini? Climate change?
Crab knew the range of
  Human love and
Fears, having
  Consumed the corpses and their brains,
Over the years, as down they'd sunk.
  From the wrack and wreck
Oh yes!
  Crab was consumed by knowledge
Which was a great advantage
  When it came to the Sea Trial—
And his carefully planned denial.

Oedipus Crab

Waiting on the slab
in the shadow of the shell hammer
the iron dream shatterer
Crab dreams of his mother.

Not much to dream of.

Crab was born
Of the sea spawn, shed, denied
from the shell womb, scattering
into the sea bleak.
Not even a kiss goodbye.

No chance to be her lover.

But then again,
Crab wasn't Greek.

—*RH, 2009.*

More 'Crab' Poems

RH to Bobbie Lamming:
Crab may or may not
become famous, but hey!
A touch of lightness in the
struggle, eh?

RH to GK: Dear Gaz, Crab is
my 'omage to Hughes. Crab
will feature often in my
madness. Crab knows all. Crab
will speak for me when my lips
are silenced.

Crab (Ghost)

Crab (ghost)
  Inspected the shell scatter
The armour shattering
  Following his capture and demise
  And claw-furious, twitchy of eyes,
God-wrathed,
  Naked in his (lack of shell)
Crab wreaked the terribleness
  Of vengeance
And hell knew no fury
  As that of crab
(Who for lunch had eaten only a very small dab).

Crab Discovers Poetry

The drowned sailor descends slowly
Towards the crusted coral
The coloured sway
Of anemone
The calcified *korallion*
Where Crab waits patiently
For the marinated meat:
His lunch, supper, afternoon tea,
(Many meals in fact;
A dead sailor goes a long way.)

And the drowned man turns—

Gently in the sea-sinking
Almost beautiful in his calm movement
A leaf falling in air
Deep below the wave heave,
Arms stretched out,
Circling down, down, through
The cold grim birth water,
His salted eyes not
crying.

Long since finished with his dying.

Shedding Leaves of Grass
And poetry by
Ted Hughes
From his pockets

The wave-torn shreds of minds,

That which was once is now, and still!
Refusing to be abandoned,
Small sockets of the brain plough.*

And though Crab (waiting) knew nothing
Of these rings, the wordplay:
After he had gorged (on sailor fat and rind)

Crab read with enthusiasm,
And learned.
New things.

And Crab decided to become a poet!

Alas,
Crab only knew eight words:

'Eat, screw, scuttle—oh fuck, a Conger eel!'

So Crab was out of luck
Wordwise. Though he didn't know it.
Didn't feel.

Yet, being Crab
Did not give up!
Sought out a Rhyme Smith on the land!
Brought the rhyme to heel.

RH (to Bobbie Lamming):
... to be continued when I
get   inspiration ... the
rhymesmith will be Garry.

(* this is in fact a very fucking
clever play on 'socket' ... as
long as you speak Anglo-
Norman. Did I just write
this? Christ, I can't believe
my own arrogance ...)

Crouched In The Sea Swirl

Crouched in the sea swirl
Coral havened
ingesting the sea's slime spawn
Crab wondered

Wandered in the crab dream,
the mind monsoon

And dreamed
Of being the first Crab
On the Moon.

How to get there. That was
Crab's problem.

There was no solution. Crab stayed
Where he was.

—RH, July 2009

Peoms

The spider in the wing-mirror of my car

lives life between peace and pandemonium.
One moment quietly spinning his net
between glass and glass,
(fisher of flies,
ignoring the windscreen banquet)
the next roaring along roadways
with windswept legs
at breathless miles-an-hour,
clinging desperately to his own image,
struggling to enter the crack
between mirror and casing.

He's learned to swear
at other spiders
speeding in Mercedes mirrors.
A well-travelled octopod,
has visited towns and cities
most bugs have never been—
Sheffield, Cardiff, Bristol, Stirling—
has webbed delicious bluebottles
on the linking motorways,
lives life on the edge of danger,
adrenaline junky of the arachnid world.

—*GK, 2010*

Ninety Nine

If I should live to ninety nine,
I'll drink a crate of good French wine,
And eat with it a leg of lamb
Followed by a juicy ham,
And a T-bone steak the size of Wales
Washed down with jugs of good real ales
And 'cause it's right to eat our greens,
There'll be a plate of *three broad beans*.
And after that it's party time,
And I'll gather the girls, those girls sublime,
(Twenty's enough) whose total age
Is a figure that cannot fit this page.
And I'll sing a saucy song or more
To all the girls of eighty-four,
And make a pass or make a date
With the prettiest lass of eighty-eight,
And stand upon a table top
And let my baggy trousers drop,
And dance the dance that Bacchus danced
When with a lass his luck he chanced,
(And they bathed in wine, to him pure heaven,
Not caring that she was eighty seven).
And then chase matron around the floor,
And after a breather, chase her more.
And run like Hell when the cops I hear,
And hope to live another year,
So I can sit, swear, laugh and curse.
And on my hundredth?
Do much worse!

—*RH, February 2008, revised later...*

Sally Dressing

(To be read aloud)

I put on these new blue genes
and felt a different person.
Around my neck, a beautiful Thai,
but I finally decided on
a collarless Irish-green *taoiseach*,
which saved embarrassment.
A pair of *petite chous*
went on my feet, with difficulty,
also coloured green.
Finally, on top of it all,
the Cote d'Azur—
which clashed with the *chous* and *taoiseach*
and was very cumbersome,
but one needs something substantial
to keep out the cold.

—*GK, 2005*

The New Brit-Lib Album By China Guesswork

For Sarah

Tracks include:

The New World of Management
The Way You Come to Know
Walking the Edge
Living in Hope, Prepared for Loss
Enlightenment by Silent Spider of the Web

(following extract from theme song; please forgive Confucius allusion; sing to music of Dylan)

'Contract runs out end of March.
Woman knows not her future. (Chorus: wailing sounds)
Then e-mail comes to another person (of woman sex) . . .
Refers to her (first mentioned woman)
As working!
On project beginning April!
Of Two Thousand
And Nine. (Chorus: sounds of salary cheque being kissed
for next few months.)'

(Confucius peotry never rhyme, by the way.)

We live in interesting times
And to the Chinese, that's a curse.
But lilacs in our dooryard bloom
And we stand in the smiles of bride and groom.
And the Wild Geese are flying south.
So what?
We never eat goose anyway.
Too expensive.
So things could be a damned sight worse.

—*RH*

Spoonering The Birds

Poodweckers hate me for playing this game
and jightnars curse my human name,
the foldginch thinks it's a terrible sin
but pipits just shake their heads and grin.

—GK, 2008

The Pasta's On

The pasta's on, I can't be seen,
I'm not forlorn
Thank fuck that Sarah's
Mowing the lawn.

Gives me time to reheat the pasta.
And scratch around for something green.

—RH, June 2009

Whether Forecast

There will be a bright star to the day,
but a band of angels is sweeping in from the West.
Later it will be Claudia.

—*GK*

A Middle-Aged Man From Kent

A middle aged man from Kent
Completely forgot it was Lent.
Went on wining and dining
Ignoring the pining.
(But that happens quite often in Kent.)

—*RH*

𝒜 Pen-pal On Another Planet

I'd like a pen-pal out in space,
don't care what colour, shape or race,
don't care if she's a he or it,
or lives inside a smoky pit,
down below the salty sea
on a swamp, up a tree.
I'd like to learn some strange new things
about my pal. Does she have wings?
Does she have flipper, claw or feather?
Is she allowed out in bad weather?
(Do her feet turn into boots
or like flowers grow some roots?)
Is her mum her dad as well?
Can she add up? Can she spel?
Does she eat jam on her bread,
or lizard's eggs, or something dead?
I'd like to know about her planet—
is it made of sponge or granite?
Are there parks and busy roads?
Do they ride on giant toads?
Does she have some kind of pet?
Would it eat me if we met?
So many things I'd like to know
about my pen-pal's world, and so,
if you hear of an address
out in the stars, out in the stars,
let me have it so I can send
Best Wishes to my unknown friend.

—GK, 2008

LIFE GOES ON...

And Peotry Persists.

Ring Of Fire

By Anon—for my friends who suffer—

Vesuvius roared!
Etna rumbles, swelling beyond the lean earth crust,
Pushing as fire pain,
The thrust with Phoenix wing,
Against the earth-skin of order.
A combat within the ring.

There is no atmospheric balm, no smoothing, of the stings,
Of the fire lust of these monsters,
Which in reverse, reverse-impale even the seats of kings.

No soothing of the rage
No calming of the hell-urn that bubbles and distends,
Swelling even the divinity of Olympus and its Gods,
Their cries denying Zeus's stealth,
Woe-begotten, far from the eyes of mortals
When their ends become the flaming portals
Of exuberance and excess, and the neglect of health.

Firestone and the Scream of Blood!
Men, Gods and Dinosaurs,
All bewildered and bemoaning the heaving, sand-scour
Of the food-flood,
Having faced the seeming passing of an asteroid.

Pity the dinosaur.
For when he lived, there was no Germoloid;
No unction,

No function to ease the pain for this poor lizard:
Other than to expose its arse
To the cold and furious blow of some Cretacious blizzard.

—RH, January 2009

Socks

Another pair of my socks
has decided to separate.
This makes seven in the last month.
Sometimes they get back together,
resolve their differences,
but too often the divorce
is permanent.

One usually stays with me,
the other runs off—
who knows where? The Sockland Islands?
It seems such a shame,
they are all so well matched.
But in the end left-right gender issues
rear their ugly feet.

—*GK*

$\mathcal{H}$ow Arcimboldo Discovered Vegetarianism

Arcimboldo opened his eyes one morning
And to his surprise
Found himself face down in a bed of fruit and veg
Being rogered by the Green Man.

He'd had an idea that something was up
(apart from the Green Man)
Because of the scent of fruit and vegetables
That had haunted his dreaming.

It had occurred to Arcimboldo
That it was too early to
Have vegetables on the table
(fruit more appropriate for breakfast time).

But Arcimboldo was stuck
(as said before)
Face down among a scattering of
Oranges, pears, apples, zucchini, pomegranates
Various root vegetables
(delicious when roasted, or even grilled)
Hosting the Green Man's penetration
And,
Whilst not being thrilled to be
Squashed into this shedding of the veg

Bore it, for
He'd got an idea, so powerful he almost fainted
Couldn't wait to paint it.

And when the Green Man had finished,
(buggered off somewhere)
Arcimboldo, without a care
For what had happened
(artists!)

Painted men covered with fruit and root.
Bloody weird to look at, but
When the Green Man's been on your case
Might as well take advantage
Of the experience and give back
The fruit in the face

And there he is—Arcimboldo
In a gallery somewhere, made of
Parsnip, citrus, fruit and shoot
A hoot? Or brilliance?
Well: testimony at least
To an inspired man's resilience.

—RH

Last Rites

First, the pathologists
of the cookhouse,
perform their autopsies
on piglets, hens and salmon,
removing the lights
during swift post mortems,
severing the bodies
into rib and joint.

Next, the undertakers
of the kitchen,
carry out obsequies
on these dead mammals, fish
and birds, in preparation
for burial in human tombs,
dressing each corpse
for the lying in state.

We file past a pheasant
looking like an Aztec
sacrifice in its cloak
of many feathers,
and a rainbow trout
embalmed in wine.
Mr Sarcophagus
looks down covetously
at each cadaver, while
Miss Funeral-Casket,
still acquiring tastes,
sends an anchovy to
its final resting-place.

After the interment,
crypts, sepulchres
and mausoleums, admire

each other's architecture,
whispering requiems
before a second laying out
and double burial,
tomb in tomb.

—*GK*

*A*cknowledgements

The following Robert Holdstock poems, published with his final novel 'Avilion', have been included in this anthology by kind permission of the Orion Publishing Group:

THE FIELD OF TARTAN
HE REGRETS THAT HIS DREAMS ARE NOT FULFILLED, YET
  DREAMS
MEMORY
THE CROSSING PLACE

THE IRON WIND first appeared in Garry Kilworth's novel 'Scarlet Sash', published by Severn House.

THE LONG DROP UPWARDS and BODY LANGUAGE first appeared in Garry Kilworth's novel 'Gemini God' published by Faber and Faber Ltd under different titles.

Many of the poems by Garry Kilworth published before 1990 appeared in 'Envoi Poetry Magazine' edited by JC Meredith-Scott.